Life Beyond Burnout

Life Beyond Burnout

Recovering Joy in Your Work

**DR. ALAN SHELTON
WITH
BETTE NORDBERG**

Life Beyond Burnout.
Copyright © 2020 by Dr. Alan Shelton, M.D., M.P.H with Beth Nordberg.

All rights reserved. No part of this book may be reproduced in any form or by any electronic or mechanical means, including information storage and retrieval systems, without permission in writing from the publisher and author, except by reviewers, who may quote brief passages in a review.

This publication contains the opinions and ideas of its author. It is intended to provide helpful and informative material on the subjects addressed in the publication. The author and publisher specifically disclaim all responsibility for any liability, loss, or risk, personal or otherwise, which is incurred as a consequence, directly or indirectly, of the use and application of any of the contents of this book.

ISBN: 978-1-952405-70-9   [Paperback Edition]
       978-1-952405-69-3   [eBook Edition]

Printed and bound in The United States of America.

Published by
The Mulberry Books, LLC.
8330 E Quincy Avenue,
Denver CO 80237
themulberrybooks.com

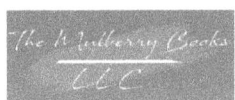

Praise for Life Beyond Burnout

Congratulations Dr. Shelton on this awesome new book! You have given an outstanding overview of the problem of burnout with practical steps and tools to deal with stress, and to recover one's joy at work. I highly recommend this book as an important resource for anyone struggling with job satisfaction. Pastors, teachers, social workers, and many more nonmedical and medical individuals could all find it life-giving, as well. Thanks for sharing your gifts, tremendous insights, stories, failures, expertise, and joy in this burnout arena with us all!

-Holle Plaehn, Pastor Emeritus at Peace Lutheran Church in Tacoma, Washington for over 40 years and author of "Plaehn Talk from the Hill"

Dr. Shelton was phenomenal. I have to admit I was in tears the first thirty minutes of his lecture. There was something about him that was deeply touching and inspiring. We have never, ever had a lecturer like Dr. Shelton visit our class. It was awesome, refreshing, and life-changing. Who knew that one could reach such a state of enlightened healing? I had never given thought to how that looks, or how to rescue myself from the dredge of burnout. Dr. Shelton should seriously consider writing a book, and/or lecturing to practitioners across the globe. His knowledge and experience are profound. I feel beyond fortunate to have him visit our class and touch our lives like he did. His lecture is truly a gift on so many levels. Thank you, and "Namaste!"

-Physician Assistant student at Pacific University, Hillsboro, Oregon, in a Lecture Evaluation response

Dr. Shelton is a favorite retreat speaker on wellbeing for young doctors in training. His vulnerability and practical wisdom enlighten us and make us more resilient.

-Dr. Kerry Watrin - Director of Tacoma Family Medicine Residency Program

Prologue

I enjoy telling stories. These days I am telling more and more of them—stories of hope and inspiration, stories I've discovered in my long journey through burnout. As I've shared my own story in presentations across the country and listened to many others, I've become even more convinced that it is possible for those who suffer from burnout to recover the joy and passion of work.

I am now the Clinical Director of the Puyallup Tribal Health Authority in Tacoma, Washington. We are a relatively large clinic providing family practice, pediatrics, internal medicine, psychiatry, dental, behavioral health and substance abuse treatment, and pharmacy services. In this busy environment, I manage my own patient load while overseeing the clinical services and staff for our organization of over 250 employees.

I would not be where I am today had I not found my way through burnout.

As a physician specializing in family practice, I began my career with the youthful zeal of the usual highly competitive, well-educated, idealistic (though inexperienced) medical doctor. Real-world medicine soon changed all that.

In my early years I worked long hours caring for patients, doing obstetrics and hospital work, managing the clinic staff, and growing my family. Over time I grew more and more dissatisfied. Though I experienced professional success and the clinic continued to grow, something critical was missing from my work life. Before long, burnout nearly sidelined me.

In the process of finding my way back, I've discovered that I was not alone. Burnout is perhaps the most pervasive quality in the work lives of those who serve the public. Today a Google search of the term *burnout* returns more than forty-two million hits. Maybe you know someone fighting with burnout. Perhaps you struggle yourself.

This book contains the story of how I've managed to recover my joy and passion—not just for my work but also for my life. Along the way, I want to share the many things I learned in the process of recovery—things about human nature, about the human brain, and about the nature of those who choose the service professions. I believe the keys I've discovered in my own recovery can help anyone suffering from professional burnout. No matter where you work, whether in education, public safety, social services, medicine, or other service professions, the simple steps I share can help you cope with the enormous pressure you face every day.

In the course of my journey, I realized that I didn't need to change careers or find another job. All along, even in my darkest days, I had always possessed everything I needed to recover joy and satisfaction—even with the extreme pressure and difficult circumstances involved in caring for an underserved population.

I just didn't know it.

Discovering the answers within myself reminds me of a story told by Russell Cromwell, founder of Philadelphia's Temple University. This story contains a powerful truth—one that can be a great gift.

Centuries ago, a rich Indian farmer owned gardens, orchards, and grain fields. Ali Hafed was both wealthy and content until one day a Buddhist priest visited Ali at his farm. In the course of their conversation, the priest described for Ali the discovery of diamonds. "A diamond is a congealed drop of sunlight," the priest explained. "With one, a man could purchase an entire continent. With a diamond mine, a man could put his children on the thrones of Europe."

This new knowledge changed Ali, though he had lost nothing and he went to bed a poor man, having discovered the poverty of discontent.

I must have a diamond mine of my own, he thought. Ali sold his farm, left his family, and used his fortune to travel the world in search of diamonds. Eventually, Ali ran out of money. Disconsolate, he threw himself into the Mediterranean Sea.

In the meantime, the farmer who purchased Ali's property went out one day to water his camel. In the garden, the camel lowered his head into a small brook. The farmer noticed a flash of light. Bending down, he discovered a beautiful black stone lying in the white sand. He brought the stone inside and displayed it on his mantel. Over the years, he found several others and added them to his collection.

Sometime later, the priest returned to Ali's farm. Entering the house, he noticed the stones and exclaimed, "Diamonds! Has Ali returned?" The new owner, certain the stone was no diamond, explained that he knew nothing of Ali's fate.

"I know a diamond when I see one," the priest exclaimed.

Together, the two men went out to the garden and dug in the sand. Before long they had discovered another stone, larger and more beautiful than the first. When the stones were evaluated, they were determined to be raw diamonds.

Ali's old farm became India's Golconda Diamond Mine, the source of Europe's most famous stones, including those of England's crown jewels, the Russian monarchy, the Hope Diamond, the Idol's Eye, and the Regent Diamond. For almost two thousand years, the Golconda mine served as the exclusive supplier of all European diamonds. Poor Ali left home to search for something that had been in his backyard all along.

Russell Cromwell used this story to inspire people to take initiative and to look into their lives and circumstances with an entrepreneurial spirit, finding their own source of wealth. His was a pull-yourself-up-by-your-bootstraps approach to building financial success. But I believe the truth of this story lies much deeper.

> Within each of us is an inner resource,
> which, when properly nourished,
> provides us with authentic peace and joy.
> These gifts are far more precious than diamonds.

Once you discover these hidden gems, you too can recover the passion and joy you once had for your work, and soar beyond burnout.

Table of Contents

Prologue vii

Chapter One:	In the Beginning 1
Chapter Two:	The Turning Point 18
Chapter Three:	Wellness 25
Chapter Four:	Stress 42
Chapter Five:	Exploring Authentic Spirituality 54
Chapter Six:	The Benefits of a Healthy Spiritual Life 61
Chapter Seven:	Mindfulness 76
Chapter Eight:	The Tool 87
Chapter Nine:	Understanding the Tool Elements 97
Chapter Ten:	Attitude: It's What We Make of It 110
Chapter Eleven:	Charting a Course: Preventing Burnout Before It Begins 122
Chapter Twelve:	Speaking the Language 136
Chapter Thirteen:	Boundaries 146
Chapter Fourteen:	The Importance of Community 158
Chapter Fifteen:	A Path to Joy 165

About the Author 175

Chapter One
IN THE BEGINNING

"In the middle of the road of my life I awoke in the dark wood where the true way was wholly lost."
Dante, *The Divine Comedy*

"I hate my job," I said. Sitting in the doctor's lounge across from my friend, I could hardly face him. "I just can't do it anymore. I can't go back."

"Isn't there *anything* you like about your job?"

I shook my head. "No," I replied, my voice breaking. "Nothing at all." I couldn't find the right words to tell him how bad things had gotten, how hopeless I felt. I no longer had the energy for my work. Cynicism had taken over my thinking.

Admitting it out loud showed me just how far I'd fallen into the dark crevasse of professional burnout. Though I had served the Puyallup Tribal Health Authority for nearly twenty years, first as a physician and more recently as medical director, I felt completely lost. I'd even begun to consider leaving medicine and giving up on the profession I loved. Could I ever escape the unending disappointment and frustration of my work? It seemed I'd been swallowed up by hopelessness.

But I hadn't always felt like that.

Twenty years before this surprising confession, I'd taken my first post-residency job as a family practice physician serving Native Americans in Tacoma, Washington. I'd begun that work full of passion, determined to make a significant difference for this underserved population. In my youthful exuberance, I expected to heal every patient and to be loved and appreciated by everyone. Instead, I encountered a population struggling with all the disadvantages of poverty and marginalization. Many suffered from the physical, social, and emotional consequences of addictive disease. Making matters worse, the staff at our medical clinic seemed to arrive and depart via some invisible merry-go-round. In my first ten years at the clinic, I had seventeen different fellow medical providers in our two physician operation.

Early on, I discovered that a tribal medical clinic is a bit like a small town. Tribal politics frequently affected organizational and clinical decisions. Supervising the medical staff required that I correct or dismiss nonperforming employees—something outside of my training and comfort zone. The work in our clinic was both emotionally and physically demanding. During those difficult years, I remember one month when I delivered eighteen babies. Early mornings, late nights, and frequent all-nighters left me chronically exhausted. But what I felt was more than physical exhaustion.

This situation of political and staff upheaval, combined with demanding and difficult patients, left me feeling fed up and frustrated. At the same time, I was exhausted, used up, empty, and hollow. I'd lost all sense of joy in my work. I had no resiliency, and I was no longer able to cope with unexpected challenges or difficulties. I had become so cynical that I no longer approached most problems in a productive way.

And then, quite suddenly, I realized that I'd begun resenting certain patients. Though I didn't feel this way about all of them, whenever a particularly difficult patient appeared on my appointment schedule, I dreaded the encounter, feeling resentful of my patient's chronic complaints, dissatisfaction, and manipulative behavior.

I just didn't want to take care of those people anymore.

Recognizing my own antipathy somehow shook me awake. It was as if by feeling this way toward my own patients, I'd crossed some invisible and unforgivable moral line. After all, I'd studied medicine in the hope that I might help suffering people. How could I have sunk so far? Overwhelmed with guilt about my attitude, my frustration mounted. At the end of the day, I had no sense of accomplishment and no job satisfaction. After a day of watching the clock, it was everything I could do to crawl back into my car and drive home.

Desperate, I tried to reverse the situation myself. Believing I suffered from fatigue, I took time off. I planned longer vacations. On weekends, I played hard—as if by wild activity I might recover my lost sense of joy and purpose. I used my time off as a way of recovering lost opportunity and lost exuberance. I coached basketball, went skiing, and spent time with my kids. I kayaked, hiked, and went camping. Those efforts, frantic as they were, made no real difference. Every Monday, I returned to work in the same condition I'd left—dreading every minute of the day ahead.

One afternoon while sitting at my desk in a common work area, a premed student came in to interview our medical staff. He approached my colleague's desk first, asking a simple question: "If you had to do it over again, would you choose to become a doctor?"

Without hesitation, the other physician replied, "No. I'd become a high school teacher and coach basketball."

Eavesdropping, I wondered how I would answer the same question. If I could go back and do it all again, would I choose medicine? What other career appealed to me?

In an instant, I knew I would choose medicine—regardless of how deeply disillusioned I'd become. When I am at my best, there is nothing quite like the work I do. When I connect with my patients, solve problems, and make a difference in outcomes, my profession provides enormous joy. Even at my lowest point, I recognized that no other work would ever satisfy me in quite the same way. At one time I'd loved my vocation, though somewhere I'd lost that sense of fulfillment. Listening to the student interview

In the Beginning

my colleague, I realized I had to find some way to turn myself around.

In the many years since that low point, my life has radically changed. I have recovered my youthful enthusiasm for the practice of medicine. But before I share the details of my recovery process, it might be helpful to explore some characteristics of burnout. See if you identify yourself in any of the symptoms or emotions described below. Have you lost your sense of professional balance or compassion? Do you find yourself with symptoms similar to depression? Has your professional malaise begun to creep into your personal life? As we explore burnout, you may feel as if you are wallowing in symptoms with which you are already far too familiar. I understand. If you need to, skip ahead to the section in chapter two titled "The End of the Beginning." There you will find the beginning of my journey beyond the misery of burnout.

CHARACTERISTICS OF BURNOUT

Burnout is often characterized by a profound loss of joy. In that way, it can be similar to depression. For some, it feels like all energy, resiliency, and satisfaction are gone from work. For others, burnout has the potential to become all-encompassing—to follow its victim home, affecting his home life, his intimate relationships, and even his physical body. For many, the symptoms of burnout remain confined to the workplace.

The medical field is especially prone to burnout, with some sources reporting burnout in one out of three health-care providers. Physicians are even more susceptible. According to *Bloomberg News* (August 20, 2013), one in two doctors report being burned out, showing signs of emotional exhaustion and little interest in work. According to the *Archives of Internal Medicine*, doctors working in emergency, family, and internal medicine are the most likely to report burnout. Though research indicates that nearly 40 percent of physicians work more than sixty hours per week, burnout is more than physical exhaustion. Burnout involves mental and emotional struggles as well. The disillusionment of burnout is so prevalent that one survey discovered that nine out of ten doctors would not recommend their profession to young people considering medicine as a career.

Of course, burnout is not limited to those in the health care professions. If you are experiencing burnout, you are not alone. As early as 1969, researchers began investigating burnout in a variety of human service professions, including health care, social work, education, and public safety. Not surprising they found that members of all these groups also struggle with the reality of burnout.

But what actually constitutes burnout?

Burnout is more than a stress-filled day. Rather, burnout is caused by experiencing persistent work-related stress day after day after day. Over time, the effects of this strain may cause a whole collection of symptoms that, when taken together, create the syndrome we describe as *burnout*. The severity of these symptoms varies widely. Not everyone is completely incapacitated by them. Most professionals experiencing burnout continue to have good days and bad days. However, as difficult experiences and stressors accumulate, people may find themselves spending more and more time battling burnout's unpleasant effects. Following are some of the common characteristics:

Exhaustion. Though burnout is frequently considered simple physical exhaustion, it is also characterized by persistent mental and emotional depletion. These symptoms, including sadness, depression, negativism, and cynicism, may coexist as well. More subtle symptoms include the loss of creativity, which inhibits innovative problem-solving. The burned-out professional is less able to cope with difficult situations because mental and emotional exhaustion inhibit the creative thinking that helps one discover solutions to presenting difficulties. By itself, exhaustion has the power to magnify the symptoms of burnout, creating a kind of downward spiral of negative emotions and hopelessness.

Detachment. One important emotional symptom of burnout is the loss of empathy. Put simply, providers of all kinds—police officers, social workers, medical providers, and teachers—simply stop being able to connect deeply and care about the people they serve. Without that concern, the burned-out employee frequently pulls away from the very relationships that make for a rewarding work life. In the case of medical workers, this includes retreating from patient interactions, which undermines the most important aspect of the doctor-patient relationship—the ability to listen to and understand the patient's difficulty. Some experts believe that by pulling away, the medical provider actually loses a key tool in patient care.

Dr. Gregory Fricchione (author of *Compassion and Healing in Medicine and Society* and former chief of psychiatry at Massachusetts General) explains the idea this way: "Empathy is like a powerful drug. It has the ability to change a patient's neurochemical ecology. If you do nothing more for your patient than to listen and care for them, though it seems small, that empathy can begin the healing process."

Though we may not admit it, medical providers frequently consider it naïve or unprofessional to be compassionate toward those we treat. Instructors and mentors in the medical professions still encourage students not to become too close to their patients. This so-called healthy distance is believed to create an objective perspective for the medical professional. However, the loss of compassion and empathy can be costly both to the patient (in terms of quality of care) and to the provider (in terms of fulfillment).

Cynicism. In the academic world, where research is dissected and critiqued with great enthusiasm, it is considered suave and sophisticated to be highly skeptical. Because medical training involves a strong focus on science and research, we approach all treatment options with a healthy dose of cynicism. We believe in and practice evidence-based medicine. Our mantra, "prove it," helps us to separate folk medicine from effective and reproducible science-based treatment. We drum scientific doubt into our medical students, elevating the attribute of skepticism to heroic proportions. As medical training progresses, professional cynicism frequently grows along with it.

Unfortunately, in the burned-out physician, that same cynicism becomes an all-consuming sentiment, pervading the doctor-patient relationship. Eventually, the burned-out provider begins to doubt or mistrust his patient's reports of pain, the history of symptoms, or his assessment of treatment results. Filtering all patient communication through the eye of detachment, cynicism and disbelief has another important, though subtle effect. These emotions and accompanying cynicism have the potential to leave the physician angry and defensive. Rather than solving problems, the burned-out physician is simply angry about *having* problems. When cynicism replaces trust, we can no longer provide adequate care.

During my worst days of burnout, one patient interaction stands out in my memory. I was with a woman whose adult son had recently died of a drug overdose. As this heartbroken mother sobbed through our interaction, I thought to myself, *I've gotta get out of here. I have two rooms full of waiting patients.*

As she cried, I found myself wondering, *What on earth did she think would happen? The kid was shooting heroin!* Instead of identifying with her grief, expressing my concern, and helping her move forward, I felt angry that she had come to me at all. My self-centered response and lack of compassion shocked me.

Loss of job satisfaction. Dr. Ray Baker, associate clinical professor at the University of British Columbia Medical School in Vancouver, Canada, and a specialist in addiction medicine, suffered his own severe burnout. As he tells it, one cool autumn afternoon, with his waiting room packed and his exam rooms full, he quietly slipped out the back door of his clinic! He had begun self-medicating his burnout with alcohol.

Dr. Baker isn't alone. Burnout is a prime factor in employee absenteeism and turnover. After a huge financial investment and many years of training, burnout has the power to put successful careers at risk. It may also contribute to the prevalent overuse of narcotics (leading to drug addiction) and alcoholism. Burnout may even contribute to suicide. According to the Association of American Medical Colleges, Sept. 2016, physician suicide may be anywhere from 40 to 70 percent higher in males and as much as 300 percent higher in females compared to the suicide rates of those in nonmedical professions.

The news about burnout can be discouraging, even dismal, but there is hope. **Burnout can actually trigger revitalization.**

It gives us an opportunity to take a closer look at how we choose to live life. Thanks to burnout, some choose another way to pursue the careers they once loved. Burnout led Dr. Baker to his passion for occupational addiction medicine. Burnout led me to the most fruitful and rewarding work of my life.

It still surprises me that the answers I discovered during my journey have changed the lives of so many. Burnout may do the same for you. Your path to recovery may reward you with new direction, renewing your old joy and passion for the very work you had come to dread.

OTHER WAYS TO DESCRIBE BURNOUT

Most experts agree that burnout is characterized by exhaustion, detachment, cynicism, and loss of satisfaction. But are there other ways of viewing the burnout experience? Do other views clarify issues which demand our attention? The following descriptions of burnout may help us recognize other factors present in our condition:

Burnout as a grief syndrome. Like me, many in the helping professions—medicine, social work, public safety, and teaching—begin their careers with a profoundly idealistic viewpoint. As they prepare for these professions, many students begin with a strong vision of their professional futures. They believe they will successfully help the people they serve, that they will be effective, and that they will make a significant difference in the world. However, once they begin their careers, the real world, full of human frailty and error, frustration and failure, leaves them disappointed at best and despairing at worst. The discrepancy between expectation and reality leaves many professionals with a deep sense of loss. According to the grief syndrome viewpoint, grief—or sadness and disappointment—arises from the death of those treasured expectations.

At one of my presentations, I was privileged to meet a young pediatrician experiencing this kind of grief. After my talk, she introduced herself with this dramatic statement: "I hate my job." She explained that the intense pressure of rushing through multiple patient interactions was nothing like the work she had visualized during her training. Her current frustration was complicated by the obligations created by her medical education.

"I can't quit," she explained. "I'm trapped. I've invested years of my life in training. I still have student loans. My family sacrificed so much for my education. There's no way out."

Experiencing the deep loss of the idealized picture she'd held during her training, she felt completely powerless to change course. I could easily identify with her situation, and I encouraged her to try some of the principles that I share in this book.

Burnout as compassion fatigue. Compassion fatigue is a way of describing what happens when professionals identify with and go out of their way to provide exceptional care for patients and clients, only to have those patients reject or walk away from their care. After investing extra time and effort to plan for the best outcome, patients or clients may abandon the well-constructed plan, leaving the care provider feeling betrayed or even abused. When patients don't appreciate their efforts—or worse, decline to participate in their own care—providers experience compassion fatigue. As a result, they are more reluctant to invest in the same way again. Unwilling to invest in other patients or clients, these providers are less likely to experience the little successes that might bring them satisfaction. In this cycle, they may lose what compassion they might have once had.

Recently one of our resident physicians experienced this kind of disappointment. She had spent significant time talking with one of her patients about a drug abuse problem and exploring options for treatment. After making numerous phone calls and asking favors of other providers, this resident eventually arranged for the patient to enter an in-patient drug treatment facility. On the day the patient was scheduled to enter treatment, he slipped out a back door of the hospital, leaving the resident feeling dismayed, disappointed, and frustrated. Her compassion had taken a big hit.

In the normal course of things, this resident would likely have pulled back from her next drug-addicted patient. She would be less likely to care about outcomes, to go out of her way, or to secure rehabilitation opportunities. Without intervention, her ability to care might have been seriously compromised. I spent a lot of time talking with her about what had happened and helping her consider another option—which I'll describe later. Our work together helped her avoid the beginning of compassion fatigue.

Burnout as cynicism. Burnout might be described as the development of a cynical worldview—a pervasively negative lens through which one views life. This was a huge part of my own problem. I often say that during my burnout I became addicted to negativity—almost as if I derived a perverse pleasure in pointing out the downside of every aspect of my day. If you could hear the things I told myself in those days, you might have heard a litany like this:

- Nothing will change.
- Nothing I do matters.
- They won't listen anyway.
- The treatment probably won't work.

Until I broke free, it was easy for me to see the shadow side of every interaction, event, and outcome. That dark viewpoint eventually permeated my soul and stole the joy from my work. My negative, doubtful viewpoint became completely pervasive, yet I did not recognize it. You might doubt the accuracy of the term *addiction*. But for me, breaking that habit involved many of the processes used in finding freedom from other addictions; it required focused work.

When cynicism characterizes your work attitude, including your attitude toward your coworkers, clients, and patients, you may be suffering from professional burnout. I believe that working from a place of cynicism guarantees you will experience the very disappointments you expect. From this negative point of view, joy and satisfaction are not possible.

Low on the energy continuum. Described this way, burnout is not a single event, a line in the sand, or an absolute lab value. Rather, this perspective views burnout as a place on an energy continuum, where one end is characterized by enthusiasm, deep work satisfaction, and joy, and the other end is characterized by exhaustion, dissatisfaction, and detachment. Most of us don't spend every day at the exact same location on this continuum. But we do tend to spend our days clustered around the same general area. In the middle of this continuum there is a broad space characterized by a general malaise. While many healthcare workers, police officers, teachers, and social workers may not be clinically burned out, they spend far too many days in this middle ground, without experiencing enthusiasm and joy in their work. It's not only care providers who suffer from this malaise; the general job market reflects many of these same issues. In a *Forbes* article on job dissatisfaction (June 2014), 52.3 percent of Americans reported being unhappy at their jobs—not exactly a rosy picture.

For some, complete burnout is kept at arm's length by intermittent satisfaction and occasional bursts of professional energy. People in this space experience seasons of dissatisfaction without recognizing the severity or significance of their symptoms. Though they may not be in full-blown clinical burnout, even those suffering from moderate dissatisfaction might benefit from the techniques we share here.

What drives the dissatisfaction experienced by so many service professionals? When I speak, I encourage my audiences to generate a list of the causes of burnout. All of my medical audiences generate a remarkably similar list:

- Demanding patients with high expectations.
- Financial issues, including productivity pressure from managers.
- The high rate of psychosocial complications in today's patient care.
- Malpractice and legal stressors.
- Frustration caused by the electronic record systems.
- Management of patient care by third-party payers (insurance companies).
- Increasing paperwork, especially in private practice.

Police officers give a similar list, citing restrictive administrations, an unappreciative public, lack of real change in repeat offenders, and the prevalence of social concerns, including family dysfunction, addiction, mental health issues, and homelessness. Teachers struggle with large class sizes, a wide range of student abilities, excessive paperwork, the demise of family stability, and uncooperative or uninvolved parents. No matter where you serve, you likely experience the chronic stress of being asked to do too much with too little.

These lists could go on and on. People have very little trouble describing what frustrates them. Most of us can easily describe our problems, commiserating as we do; we just can't solve them. I promise, in the course of this book, we will explore important techniques that will help us cope with these demanding and frustrating difficulties.

CAUSES OF BURNOUT

So far, we've considered ways of viewing burnout. Now let's explore the underlying causes of burnout. Here are four of the most widely held ideas. In my opinion, burnout is most likely caused by a combination of these factors:

Lack of control. As much as we struggle to provide the best care—by establishing clear responsibilities and describing clear goals and visions—the truth remains that few professionals have any control over outcomes. We simply cannot predict which students will accept the challenge, which gang members will turn their lives around, or how disease processes will respond to standardized treatment. Will the student do the homework? Will an arrest motivate this young person to make real changes? Will therapy help this family? Will the parent undergo drug treatment? Will my patient's body overcome the infection? Will the chemotherapy overcome the cancer?

Most of the time, in spite of our best efforts, the outcome is out of our hands.

At the same time, we cannot control whether patients, students, or clients will follow our advice or recommendations. Will the patient stop drinking? Will they begin an exercise program? Will they restrict sugar? We can only provide our best suggestions and hope for the best. When others refuse to respond, our hard work can feel wasted and unproductive.

Other aspects of work lie beyond our control as well. Most health-care providers, social workers, teachers, and public safety personnel work under the direction of others. Frequently, these directors are untrained in the very areas of expertise they supervise. Business managers and administrators design policies and programs. Insurance companies and regulatory bodies often direct client care and billing. Politicians may supervise police management and firefighting services. Frustrations mount when untrained supervisors direct much of our work.

Health care is no different. Administrators frequently determine the number of patients we see, the types of patients we treat, and the choice of electronic record technology. They control the amount of time we spend with clients or patients and the kinds of treatments we provide. Those who design electronic records may not have a medical background. This nonmedical oversight is especially true of insurance companies, where account managers, not medical professionals, often determine medical care. Frustration inevitably results when we are not authorized to provide the care we believe is best for our patients or clients.

This same struggle exists among police and safety officers who often serve under the direction of political appointees. I know firefighters who serve under town councils who have reduced shift size and closed fire stations. These firefighters believe they are being asked to risk their lives protecting people and property without the proper support staff needed to ensure their own safety.

Teachers and school administrators work under the supervision of public school boards whose members may or may not have classroom experience. School boards may make decisions based on political expediency and finances rather than what is best for those in classroom front lines, leading to overcrowding, unreasonable behavior management policies, and unrealistic performance expectations. Teachers working in the same district may face and struggle with wide disparity in the quality of buildings, equipment, and student abilities in high-income versus low-income areas.

This lack of control can set the stage for chronic frustration—the chronic stress syndrome we've described—which may deteriorate into full blown burnout.

The suppression of emotion. In many helping professions, we are trained to avoid becoming emotionally attached to the patient or client. This professional distance is believed to help us to make wise professional treatment choices (avoiding potential legal and malpractice issues) and protect us from the potential emotional injury caused by grief. The problem with this training is that it may lead professionals to grow less and less empathetic over time.

Without empathy, compassion diminishes, and we are less likely to engage our patients. New evidence suggests that the lack of compassion diminishes the quality of patient care.

And, some believe that a lack of emotional engagement hurts the professional as well. According to an article in the *Journal of Participatory Medicine* (April 2012), connecting with patients gives greater meaning to providers' work and actually *prevents* burnout. Without empathy and connection, even successful outcomes generate less satisfaction for the provider. When a health-care professional is less engaged, he or she cannot own and celebrate the little victories of patient issues. Without celebration, work satisfaction takes a hit, leaving providers even more prone to burnout.

Perfectionism. The intensity and competition of students hoping to enter the medical professions, especially those studying to become physicians, self-selects people with high performance and achievement standards. These students learn quickly, test well, and aspire to success. Highly self-critical, this group tends toward perfectionism, sharing a performance-oriented viewpoint. These students expect all interactions, treatment protocols, and interventions to go well. When they don't, these professionals may obsess on failures, even relatively small ones. In a day when nine things go well, the perfectionist will concentrate on the one thing that went badly, often acquiring a sense of inadequacy or guilt that leaves them feeling strongly dissatisfied with their role.

I am not immune to this tendency. Whenever I lecture, I have my audience fill out feedback forms. In nearly every case, I receive positive reviews from health care professionals who deeply appreciate talks preparing them for the realities of the work they have chosen. However, I always have at least one review from someone who did not like my presentation. Which review catches my attention? When I find myself feeling defensive, I have to remind myself of the many people who appreciate my work. Like so many in my profession, I too expect perfection.

Workaholic tendency. In the course of their extensive training, high-achieving individuals become comfortable with delayed gratification. Willing to invest large amounts of time learning to do their work well, many in the helping professions derive their value and personhood from successfully completing difficult assignments. This strong drive to produce and accomplish may leave these professionals vulnerable to unhealthy boundaries.

Many spend more time at work than they invest in healthy relationships. For some, they so closely identify with their roles (for instance as a doctor, a nurse, a counselor, or a police officer) that the role itself becomes their *only* identification. As this role crowds out other parts of their lives, these highly driven individuals eventually feel most at home in the work environment. Should that work become less satisfying, the significance of burnout is amplified. The burned-out workaholic has few options.

Some blame workaholism on poor personal boundaries. Working with many other physicians, I am frequently asked to cover for my coworkers. I remember one example when a coworker called asking me to take his night on call. At the time, I had my own obligations, but because of a sense of duty, of team play, or perhaps of obligation, I felt forced to agree. As that night on call expanded into a busy night, spent largely at the hospital, I found my resentment toward my coworker growing with every patient interaction. I felt stuck—or worse, used. My resentment did not enhance my care for those patients, and without help, those emotions might have moved me even deeper into burnout.

High-performing individuals serving in high-stress positions create a nearly perfect storm for producing burnout. Our lack of control, suppression of emotions, along with tendencies toward perfectionism and overwork, can accelerate the burnout process as gasoline accelerates fire.

But there is hope. Burnout can also be a trigger, an opportunity to reassess and reevaluate. Burnout can help us find what Dante described as the "true way." I know; I found my way back. You can too.

Chapter Two
THE TURNING POINT

"What we know matters but who we are matters more."
Brené Brown, *Daring Greatly: How the Courage to Be Vulnerable Transforms the Way We Live, Love, Parent, and Lead*

WHO AM I REALLY?

In the midst of my own crisis, during the days I dreaded getting out of bed and resented going to work, I began asking some important questions. Every morning as I hit the snooze button over and over, I buried my head under the covers, wondering: *Who am I, really?*

I knew that I was more than my body. The face in my bathroom mirror reminded me that time marched on. No matter how I felt on the inside, I couldn't deny the white hair and added weight. I was no longer the man of my youth. Somehow, I understood that the real me was more than the aging face I shaved every morning.

And I had to be more than my job—more than the roles I filled in life. Though I'd loved it at first, my job had begun to crush the life out of me. Still, my position symbolized accomplishment and status. If I were nothing more than my job, why was I so miserably unhappy, so dissatisfied? I had to be more than a doctor, a father, a husband, a coach, and a son. Though I filled each of these positions, the real me was something deeper and more meaningful. But what? No matter how much I tried, I couldn't get to the bottom of the nagging question. "Who am I, really?"

Others struggle with these same issues. Our American culture rarely encourages us to ask deep questions of ourselves, let alone look for truthful answers. It seems as if we are driven to keep moving so that our frenetic activity keeps us from doubting the system that leaves us feeling so alone and depleted. In the end, I've discovered that many of the really important answers lie deeply hidden—even from ourselves.

Our society provides several shallow and largely artificial answers to the question, "Who am I, really?":

You are what you own. Brand names. Luxury cars. Elegant, oversized homes. Yachts. Even my wristwatch is meant to send a message about my identity and value. Sixty-second commercial breaks reinforce the lesson: our value as people lies in our possessions. When we believe this lie, we focus on how we appear to others. The belief drives us to accumulate and protect our stuff.

Yet, most of us understand that we are far more than what we own. Deep down, we know that the poorest person in Ethiopia is no less valuable than Bill Gates or Warren Buffet. At its root, this answer—that we are what we own—is insufficient.

You are what you do. In nearly every introduction or conversation, we ask strangers, "What do you do?" A person's career can be the source of immense pride or the source of a subtle, almost nagging shame. In times of economic crisis, I've heard of unemployed CEOs, even those desperate for jobs, who refuse to accept new jobs with less prestige than their old positions, even when no other options were available. Parents who leave high-paying jobs to stay at home with their children often report difficulty with self-esteem and satisfaction, even when they believe they have made the best choice for themselves and their families.

In truth, we are much more than what we do. There was a time, before you became a doctor, a teacher, or a firefighter, that you were a young person of value. There will be a season, after your career ends, when you will be a person of age and wisdom. You are more than your job—far more than any role you will ever fill.

You are what other people say about you. This is perhaps the subtlest of the many identity lies. Rarely do we actually know what others are saying *about* us. We are far more aware of how they respond and what they say *to* us. Still, most of us to go to extreme lengths in order to please others.

If we believe that we are nothing more than what others say or think about us, we fall into another trap. Driven for the approval of others, we may begin to compromise our personal values. In the end, we distort ourselves to fit some false image we have conjured up, behaving only to satisfy those we hope to please. In the process, we become someone we hardly recognize. Keeping up the act, feeding the approval cycle takes huge amounts of energy. In the end, it creates a kind of stress all its own.

When we believe these three lies—that we are what we own or what we do or what others say about us—we take on even larger burdens, endlessly driven to accumulate stuff, to seek higher or more prestigious positions, and to please others. In the end, we are nothing more than puppets, dancing at the end of someone else's powerful strings. Seeking possessions, positions, or approval, we are less able to set healthy boundaries with those who would use and discard us. During those days of misery and questioning, I recognized that in many ways, I had bought into these American lies. Now, they were threatening to crush me.

THE END OF THE BEGINNING

During my darkest days, I believed that I'd successfully hidden my struggle from my clinic staff. I was wrong. Though they didn't say much, they recognized that I was no longer the Dr. Shelton they knew and loved. I'd become a cranky, difficult coworker. Though they gave me more space, they didn't give up on me. In fact, my clinic staff actually initiated the surprising appointment that changed my life.

One morning, in the midst of a busy schedule, I took a call from a psychologist in our behavioral health clinic. "Dr. Shelton," she began, "the Native traditional healer is here today. He has a vacancy at noon. Would you like to take the appointment?" I tried to avoid the encounter. "I appreciate your concern," I hedged. "I think we have a noon department meeting." I looked up from the phone to see my clinic nurses shaking their heads as they mouthed, "No meeting." Suddenly, the picture became crystal clear: I'd been set up; I was stuck.

I'd never spoken to this psychologist about my difficulty with burnout. Though I hadn't told anyone at work about my struggles, clearly my coworkers knew more than I suspected. Worse, I realized they must have been talking about me.

Boxed in, my obligation to my staff demanded I go. After all, they were only trying to help. Reluctantly, I agreed to take the appointment with the traditional healer. The awkward phone call left me feeling embarrassed.

As the hour approached, my anxiety grew. I tried to rationalize; after all, how bad could it be? I'd never considered visiting a healer, a shaman, or a medicine man. Though some of my patients saw them, I didn't even know what they did. I was skeptical; really, how could a Native healer help me?

Maybe I'd have a chance to talk about my problem and gain some insight.

At noon, I entered a small room where Doby, an elderly gentleman in a Pendleton vest, sat at a small table. He wore his white hair in a crew cut. Behind him stood his middle-aged son who had a wispy beard and long ponytail. The younger man held a Native hand drum. The healer looked up from the list before him, surprised to see me. "Dr. Shelton!" he exclaimed, obviously taken aback by a visit from the Clinical Director of the Health Authority.

"In order for me to help you," he explained, "you must believe in spiritual things." He seemed doubtful that a non-Native trained in Western medicine could be open to spiritual things.

"Oh, I'm good there," I said. "I grew up in a religious home." At the time, I had little understanding of true spirituality.

He nodded. "So how can I help?"

I hesitated, unsure where to start. "It is getting really difficult to come to work," I said.

He put up his hand, and then slowly, with great detail, the healer told a long story about his own father. As the tale continued, I realized that I was not going to have a chance to say anything at all about my issue. Talking about my difficulty and gaining some insight had been the one thing I thought might help. This was clearly not a part of the healer's treatment plan.

The long story grew longer. He told about his father's passing from this world into the next—interrupted periodically by his son, who suddenly sang out as he played the hand drum. Before long, I realized that these outbursts underscored significant parts of the story, though I did not understand their importance. Politely, I waited for them to finish.

Eventually, Doby stood and walked around the table. He stood behind me. "I will see what I can do," he said. Then he began to sing a Native chant, which his son accompanied on the hand drum.

As he sang, I realized that this was the treatment, and I found myself silently praying, "Make it work!" By this point, I was so desperate for change that I was willing to take any help I could get—even from a shaman.

Abruptly, he stopped singing and proclaimed, "Your spirit was gone. I put it back."

In my skeptical frame of mind, the statement struck me as amusing. *Where had it gone?* I wondered. I didn't feel anything. Not wanting to appear disrespectful, I decided not to ask questions. Instead, I graciously thanked the healer and his son and left the building. As I walked across the parking lot to my own clinic, I reflected on the experience. I decided to call the encounter a learning experience. At least now I understood what occurred when my patients went to the healer. I returned to work with the expectation that nothing had changed—that is, until I began seeing patients.

That afternoon, I had the overwhelming sense that I was again at my best. I moved from patient to patient, feeling the flow, listening, connecting, responding, and solving problems. My creative energy felt spot on. Even when my staff discovered a double booking with a difficult patient, I quickly came up with a satisfactory solution.

At one point, I stepped out of an exam room to an empty office. "Where is everyone?" I asked.

"They're gone," my nurse said. "That was your last patient."

Astounded, I wondered how that could have happened. During the past several years at the tribal clinic, I'd never needed anyone to tell me when my day was over.

The next morning at our staff meeting I announced to everyone, "I'm back!" I even admitted that I'd gone to see the healer. "He put my spirit back," I explained. For a few days I continued to experience the same creative energy, connecting with my patients as I experienced the old joy of practicing medicine again. It felt wonderful to return to my old and best self.

Unfortunately, the renewal lasted only a couple weeks.

And then things spiraled downward again. Disappointed, I wondered what to do. I certainly couldn't keep going back to the healer every two weeks. Part of me was ashamed. I had no clue why the healer's treatment had worked or what had gone wrong in the weeks since I'd seen him. Yet, I believed he'd given me an important clue: "Your spirit was gone. I put it back."

The healer's words rang over and over in my mind. As I considered them, I had to admit that I'd made little effort to nurture or care for my own spiritual life. Though I understood the requirements for keeping a healthy body, I'd never been concerned for my spiritual health. I began to see that I'd received more from the interaction with the Native healer than I first understood. Because of that encounter, I recognized that something important was missing in my life. I began to wonder if most of the responsibility for my burnout was mine. Perhaps this missing spiritual element was somehow key to my condition.

I recognized my need to explore this issue of spiritual health. Driven to answer these and other questions, I arranged a three-month leave of absence. In my mind, I envisioned this time spent in a short but purpose-driven sabbatical.

Over those months, I made it my goal to read, journal, and explore. I was determined, no matter what my search might entail, to discover how to develop and maintain a healthy spiritual life—one that would help me recover my joy and forever protect me from the unhappiness and frustration of burnout. Now, so many years later, I'm certain that I've found some of the answers.

Chapter Three
WELLNESS

"You can no more wish spiritual health into existence than you can wish physical health into existence."
Lance Witt, *Replenish: Leading from a Healthy Soul*

The more I considered the words of the Native healer—that my spirit was gone and he'd put it back—the more they made sense. In the course of my education and advanced training, I *had* lost connection with any genuine spirituality I might once have enjoyed. During my sabbatical, I began to dig into this concept of a healthy spiritual life, reading books, listening to experts, pondering deep questions of my own. Was there a connection between burnout and spirituality? What did it mean to be spiritually healthy? Could I nurture my own spirituality in a more meaningful and effective way? Could I ever return to that best self I'd known so long ago? If I did, how would I make it last?

As I considered these questions, I remembered a Native American wellness workshop I'd once attended. In this presentation, wellness had been defined not by the absence of disease but instead by the manifestations of a balanced life, a life in harmony, and a life lived with a sense of wholeness or peace. Described this way, wellness could coexist with chronic disease, provided the disease itself was well managed.

This kind of wellness is not defined by lab results. It is revealed in our attitudes, behaviors, and responses to difficult people and situations. Described this way, one living in a state of wellness, or balance, is both poised and resilient. A balanced person can keep his or her cool, possessing positive energy even in the face of deep frustration. A balanced life enables us to function at optimum levels.

In Native American thought, this idea of balance, or wellness, is illustrated by the Wellness Circle, where one large circle represents the entire individual life. Inside this large circle the four directions are depicted. Among other things, the four directions represent physical, emotional, mental, and spiritual health. In this model, wellness is achieved through balance and vigor in each of the individual parts. Our English language affirms this concept using descriptive words for health in these four areas:

- When our bodies are healthy, we say we are physically fit.
- When our minds are healthy, we say we are mentally stimulated.
- When our emotions are healthy, we say we are well-adjusted.
- When we are spiritually healthy, we say we are connected.

Though each of these parts is unique, they overlap in that the struggles of one area may cause other areas to suffer. From experience, I already understood that burnout had affected all of me—my body, my mind, and my emotions. This interconnectedness can confuse our approach to treating burnout. Because burnout causes fatigue, many address burnout by adding rest or taking more time away from work. Some treat the emotional consequences of burnout with antidepressants. Many attempt to recapture the emotional energy lost to burnout with sabbaticals, vacations, and long weekends. I'd tried these approaches myself, taking long breaks away from the clinic. During my time away, though I played hard, I returned to the clinic exhausted but hopeful that things might be different. After only a day or two, my misery returned in full force.

A lack of intellectual stimulation (leading to mental boredom) can also contribute to burnout. This is observed in those working highly repetitive jobs. Consider the manufacturing industry where redundancy denies workers mental stimulation and creativity. Here, some people experience a kind of boredom so severe that it may also lead to burnout. In this way, surprisingly, police work and manufacturing jobs can lead to similar frustrations.

Mike, a Toledo policeman, told me that burnout frequently follows endless days of repetitive policing tasks. "We do the same things day after day. We go to the same homes. We arrest the same people. We don't think; we follow rules. Nothing changes. No one decides to change. It's mind-numbing." After only seven years on the force, Mike had already begun studying to change professions.

Burnout frequently bleeds into other areas of our lives. In my case, the people I love had grown tired of my endless complaining. Burnout bled into my relationships with my family.

The more I considered this idea of balanced wellness and spiritual health, the more convinced I became that my spiritual health would play a vital role in recapturing my best self. It was as if a light bulb came on. A big part of my unhappiness was undoubtedly connected to the atrophy—weakness—of my spiritual life. This imbalance had affected my work life, throwing my whole being into disarray. It reminded me of the powerful words of Jesuit priest and French philosopher Pierre Chardin: **"We are not human beings having a spiritual experience. We are spiritual beings having a human experience."**

I began to understand that caring for my spiritual health wasn't optional; it was critical. According to Chardin, my spirit wasn't just a small part of me as I had believed. Instead my spirit *was* me—in my most genuine form. As I internalized this concept, I experienced a remarkable paradigm shift.

RELIGION AND SPIRITUALITY

You may assume that when I speak of spirituality I am speaking of religion. I am not. Though spirituality and religion are intertwined, they are not equal. Spirituality is a way of connecting to and understanding the realm of human experience that is larger than any one of us—larger than what we can see and feel and measure. It encompasses our connection to the Divine. True spirituality precedes religion, in that I must be awake to spirituality before I can experience the joy of religious tradition.

Where the spirit is awake, religion may follow. Religion is a way of codifying the spiritual experience. It is a way of celebrating spirituality by giving order, language, and ceremony to the spiritual. Religion can be an important bridge to, or affirmation of, our spirituality. It can help us feel connected to the Divine and to others, but it also has the power to separate us from others. Religion can leave us feeling superior, judging people in a way that divides us from one another. On its own, religion can even leave individuals with guilt that actually separates them from the Divine.

True spirituality is much harder to measure than religious form. True spirituality brings compassion and empathy. It opens us to an awareness of the Divine's presence and to its guidance. Because spirituality cannot always be defined or quantified, it leaves us open to the deeper mysteries of faith. I would say that all great spirituality is ultimately about letting go—about trust or faith. It is about serving rather than managing.

This contrast, between quantification and mystery, is especially difficult for those of us in the medical profession. Many of us remain focused on the physical, the tangible, and the quantifiable. We operate based on the scientific method. For us, the idea of personal spirituality, which defies scientific modalities, can be very difficult. Along the path of science we are logical, analytical, and, above all, rational. We are taught to deny mystery, awe, and the things of the spiritual realm because these things defy quantification.

This bias toward the concrete and measurable extends to our larger culture as well. No matter what trial society faces, people look confidently to science for solutions. AIDS? Find a vaccine. Earthquakes? Develop an early warning system. Global warming? Build an electric car. Our scientific overconfidence leaves us out of balance and spiritually undernourished.

In a famous quote often credited to Albert Einstein, Bruce Cameron recognized this weakness in our thinking, writing in his 1963 volume, *Informal Sociology*, "**Not all that is counted counts. Not all that counts can be counted.**"

This idea that we are more than cells and synapses has also been fully embraced by neuroscientist and surgeon Dr. Eben Alexander, former Harvard Medical School faculty member, researcher, and private clinician. Alexander, who believed that all consciousness depended on a fully functioning brain, experienced his own life-changing event—one that challenged his most deeply held assumptions. In 2008, when a rapidly progressing E. coli meningitis suddenly struck Alexander, he was admitted to the ICU in a coma and placed on a ventilator. During this time, doctors deemed Alexander's brain nonfunctional, documented by various CAT scan, blood, and bioelectric tests.

And yet, during the seven days that his condition continued to deteriorate, something dramatic happened. Once he regained consciousness, Alexander related vivid memories of his experiences during the coma. Today he insists that the world he encountered during his coma was more real and genuine than the physical reality we all experience every day. This remarkable life occurred when Alexander's brain was deemed completely nonfunctional. He had experienced a kind of consciousness even with a nonfunctioning brain.

His conclusion—that consciousness is more than cellular and neuroelectric science can explain—has driven Alexander to new research. You can read more about this story in his book *Proof of Heaven* (Simon and Schuster, 2012). We are, Alexander claims, far more than brain biology.

Dr. Stanislov Grof's writings are in agreement. A psychiatrist working at the Maryland Psychiatric Research Center in Baltimore, Dr. Grof was awarded the 2007 Vision 97 award for his research on nonordinary states of consciousness. In his acceptance speech, given in Prague, this physician, with more than fifty years of research, said this:

Materialistic science does not have a place for any form of spirituality and considers it to be essentially incompatible with the scientific world view. It perceives any form of spirituality as a lack of education, superstition, gullibility, primitive magical thinking, or a serious psychopathological condition. **Modern consciousness research shows that spirituality is a natural and legitimate dimension of the human psyche and of the universal order of things.**

You may test this theory by trying this simple visualization exercise: Imagine for a moment that you are able to attend your own funeral. Imagine lying in your coffin while others, friends, relatives, and work associates, celebrate your life. With this picture in mind, ask yourself this question: What matters most to you, right now?

I completed this guided exercise during one of my own counseling sessions. To my surprise, what mattered most to me was that my sons should know that I loved them. Though I have one daughter, my deepest concern was for my sons. Thinking about this, I believed that my daughter understood my love, convinced by my actions toward her. But I had treated my boys differently. Did they know that I loved them? As I thought about my funeral, I had no concern for titles or publications and no worry about professional status or accomplishments. Instead, I worried most about those I loved.

This exercise points us toward what truly matters in life, toward the eternal, and toward those things that might last even after our physical lives are over. Most of us recognize that the lasting, or eternal, parts of our lives center around issues like love, service, and wisdom. These values outlast us. These things truly count. Spirituality is that part of us that brings purpose and meaning to our work, our relationships, and our lives. Because spirituality focuses on the intangible, we find it difficult to measure. Kindness, love, and wisdom cannot be quantified.

Mother Teresa believed that humans were created for more than our work—more than our contributions to society. She believed that we were created to love and be loved. One of Mother Teresa's favorite wise quotes that my wife and the mother of our six children has had as a mantra on our kitchen wall for decades, illustrates this further: "Do small things with great love."

Through our emphasis on science, many of us have lost our connections to intuition, wisdom, experience, and spirituality. Ideally, medical professionals should be able to integrate science and spirituality, for each complement the other. After my experience with the Native healer, for a short season, I found myself doing my best work again. Somehow, I needed to nurture my spirituality in a way that provided prolonged change.

Perhaps you have begun to wonder about your own spirituality. You might begin assessing your spiritual health by answering these questions:

- Do I experience empathy? Do I have genuine connections with others?
- Am I able to sit quietly, feeling connected to something bigger than myself?
- Do I experience moments of transcendence—moments when I am deeply aware of something bigger, something more significant, and something far beyond my normal state?

- Do I have a connection with the Divine (however I define it)?
- Do I live a quiet inner life, trusting something bigger than myself?
- Am I able to let go of frustrations, disappointments, the need to win, and the need to be right?
- Do I feel called to service?

As I studied, I began to recognize that the true proof of spirituality lies in our ability to expand our hearts toward loving-kindness, compassion, and empathy. Though this includes my thinking and behaviors, my spirituality goes beyond these things and into something deeper. How could I grow my spirit in this broad yet practical way?

Though I did not yet fully understand this concept of spiritual health or connectedness, I did know something about physical fitness. As a longtime basketball coach and competitive runner, I understood how to build physical health. Achieving physical fitness involves a fairly routine list of commitments:

- Regular exercise: building strength and endurance contributes to fitness.
- A healthy diet: eating well contributes to fitness.
- Avoiding bad habits protects fitness (smoking, alcohol, overeating, excess sugar, etc.).

Might these commitments have corollaries in the spiritual realm? I decided to see if this three-step pattern might also serve to build spiritual fitness. If I could incorporate similar spiritual habits, perhaps I could grow my own spirituality. As I pondered this idea, I remembered something I'd observed at the Native American wellness conference where I'd first considered the idea of wellness.

As participants, we'd been assigned to small groups. In my group, an older man—who seemed very wise—garnered the attention of the younger members. They gave him great respect, deferring to his judgment. At one point, a young man asked him, "Are you a medicine man?"

"No," he said. "But every morning I begin my day talking to the Creator, thanking him for a new day. I ask the Great Spirit for wisdom to live well that day."

As he spoke, I remembered that I'd observed him during my morning run on the campus. He sat quietly on the grass, obviously in the midst of his prayer practice. While I was doing my physical exercise, he was doing his spiritual exercise. He was living at least one prerequisite of spiritual fitness. I decided it was time to incorporate that same kind of regular practice into my daily habits.

DAILY SPIRITUAL EXERCISE.

Because we are all unique, this habit will look different for every person. I advise you to discover your own spiritual exercise rather than copy those belonging to someone else. Choose a moment to get beneath the busyness of your day. Open your heart and see what transpires. I begin my daily spiritual exercise with gratitude.

In one story of Native American prayer, a child asks his grandfather about prayer. "Thank you," said the old man, "is the only prayer you need to know." The child asked him to explain. He replied, "If I only ask for things, I talk too much. In asking, I shut down my connection with the Divine."

In my childhood, I believed that prayer consisted of talking and asking. I've come to understand that though these are important aspects of prayer, they are activities of the mind. By concentrating on lists and requests, I avoid the most important benefit of prayer, which is renewal. In the same way that I must plug in my cell phone to replenish its battery, so I must plug into the Divine's presence in order to restore my own power.

For me, gratitude primes the spiritual pump. After a few moments, I invite the Divine's presence to join me. I breathe deeply, focusing only on my own breathing. As I tune into the Divine's presence, I try to avoid words. Instead, I allow thoughts to come and go without intervention; I am aware of these thoughts without judging them.

I take time to be fully present and fully aware. At this point, I may open a book and read inspiring words of spiritual reflection. Then I might meditate on some aspect of what I have read. After this, I might make requests of the Divine. Beginning my day in this way, I reaffirm that I am a spiritual being—not a human doing.

A HEALTHY SPIRITUAL DIET.

When I speak to my patients about a healthy diet, I explain that the human body needs proper nutrition in order to operate at its best. The same is true for the spirit. In the same way that a diet of junk food, candy, pop, and sugar will surely impair physical fitness, spiritual fitness may also be blocked by unhealthy intake.

George Bernard Shaw shares a well-known Native American story about the idea of a spiritual diet this way: A grandfather speaking to his young grandson says, "Inside me are two wolves always fighting. One is angry and bitter. The other is good, kind, and gentle."

His grandson asks, "Which wolf wins?"

The grandfather replies, "The one I feed the most."

Thinking about this story, I considered my own habits. Often, in the midst of my season of burnout, I came home from work frustrated and tired. After dinner, I collapsed into my favorite chair, clutching the television remote. As I channel surfed through the evening, I thought I was relaxing. But was I really? In those images, I fed myself a steady diet of violence, dissatisfaction, greed, and seduction—all of it heavily peppered with a wide variety of vulgar characters and activities.

As I thought about my television diet, I recognized that very little of it was relaxing. Rarely did it feed my spirit. Instead, I was living the vicarious fight-or-flight responses of some highly improbable story line—as if it were my own. No wonder when I went to bed I would lie awake long into the night.

Instead how might I have chosen to feed my spirit? There are so many avenues available. Music is often called the window to the soul. It elevates and inspires us. So does great literature. Religious ceremony can also help us to connect and feed our spirits. Inspirational reading has the power to do the same. Naturalist John Muir felt that nature helps people connect and strengthen their souls, writing, "Everybody needs beauty … places to play in and pray in where nature may heal and cheer and give strength to the body and soul alike."

Feeding the spirit rarely happens by accident—any more than a nutritious dinner accidently appears on my dinner table. As my wife reminds me, healthy dinners take time to plan, purchase supplies, and prepare. If I want to feed my spirit well, I must provide myself spiritual opportunities, making good spiritual food a regular part of my daily life.

AVOIDING BAD HABITS.

In my medical practice, I do more than diagnose and treat illness. I try to promote healthy living. Unfortunately, I must also spend a lot of time encouraging my patients to let go of bad habits. Bad physical habits, such as smoking, overeating, and sedentary lifestyles, are all linked to debilitating illness. Bad habits can also inhibit spiritual health. In the realm of the soul, I've uncovered three major habits that can contribute to spiritual malaise:

Complaining. Research shows that complaining is a common habit. In fact, some studies report that as much as 75 percent of our conversation might be categorized as complaining, with most of us complaining more than seventy times every day. Though a little grumbling doesn't seem too harmful, it can be. Complaining keeps us from gratitude, which I believe is one of the central premises of spiritual peace and health.

You may think that you are different and that you don't complain that much. I did too, at least until a friend challenged me to count the number of times I complained in a single day. Being a competitive person, I believed that I didn't complain as much as the average Joe. On the appointed day of my challenge, my alarm went off. I groaned aloud as I reached over to hit the snooze button. Then I remembered: *Today is the day I count my complaints.* By groaning, I had already complained and I hadn't even gotten out of bed! I went over to the window and opened the drapes. It was raining. *Oh no,* I thought, *another rainy day.* Complaint two. I shook my head. With the rest of the day to improve, I headed for the bathroom. I stepped into the shower, enjoying the hot water over my back, when suddenly the water turned cold. Indignant, I jumped out, aware that my son had flushed the downstairs toilet. Taut with frustration, I grabbed a towel. Abruptly, I realized: complaint three.

Before I'd even dressed, I waved my inner white flag. That brief experiment opened my eyes. I spent too much of my day frustrated by and complaining about every inconvenience and interruption—including my blaring alarm clock, rainy skies, crowded waiting rooms, overwhelming paperwork, noncompliant patients, and staff disagreements. Unaware of the consequences, I had let these irritations generate a complaining habit, which progressed unchecked until accumulated stresses laid me low. By my own volition, I bathed myself in a nearly constant bath of fight-or-flight hormones. No wonder I experienced exhaustion and burnout.

My little experiment also showed me that it wasn't enough to simply recognize my bad habit. If I wanted to build spiritual health and connectedness, I somehow needed to change it. My habit was so firmly entrenched that only real effort would overcome it. The key, I discovered, was to focus on gratitude. Meister Eckhart, German philosopher and theologian, said, "If the only prayer you ever say in your entire life is thank you, it will be enough." St. John of Kronstadt affirmed this principle, saying, "Prayer is a continual state of gratitude," and, "Gratitude is the heart of prayer."

I began to battle my complaining habit by keeping a thankfulness journal. At first, my gratitude was shallow, but I use the term low hanging fruit. You can always be grateful that your situation is not worse or that you have an opportunity to grow and learn from the difficulty. So I began by being grateful for having a job and grateful that not all of my patients were difficult. I was grateful for my family. From this small beginning, I gradually grew a more sophisticated awareness of the goodness I experienced.

Cultivating gratitude, I recognized remarkable convergences in my world. People came to see me at precisely the right time. Ideas and solutions presented themselves at opportune moments. My gratitude grew with these convergences. At the same time, I observed the Divine breaking into my world in new and delightful ways. This might occur in the glistening of rain on dark green leaves or sunlight gleaming off wet pavement. The divine breakthrough might occur in a glorious sunset or the smile of a young child. I began to feel gratitude for these moments as well. The more I focused on gratitude, the more I found for which to be grateful. My heart felt lighter as I complained less and gave thanks more. Gratitude quieted my complaining habit.

Resentment. I discovered another habit inhibiting my spiritual health. Resentment had the power to squelch any connection I might make with the Divine. Many have quoted the famous line, "Resentment is like drinking poison hoping the other person will die." In fact, metaphysician Florence Scovel Shinn said, "Lack of forgiveness is the greatest cause of all disease, so much so that one should not be asked '*What* is wrong with you?' but instead, '*Who* is wrong with you?'"

I don't yet ask this question of my patients. But I have treated many physical illnesses that are closely related to resentment, anger, and unforgiveness. Many of the young men I see are angry about absent fathers. Others are bitter about the racial injustices they face. Living in a river of negative emotions has the power to cause great physical, emotional, and spiritual harm. I treat many of these secondary ailments—high blood pressure, headaches, backaches, and addictions—every day in our clinic.

Forgiveness—letting go of our injuries and releasing those who have hurt us—is the best cure for resentment. In forgiveness, we experience freedom that opens us to connection, both with others and with the Divine. Forgiveness is an act of the heart that brings peace to both the mind and body.

I find it easier to extend forgiveness when I realize that most people act out of the hurts and deficits of their past. In some cases, poor parenting, difficult circumstances, and poor modeling leave patterns that surface in the way people interact. In many cases, the people who hurt me have not experienced the same kind of love and nurturing that I have. For them, an emotional poverty is expressed in a poverty of character. Recognizing this does not negate the injury they may have caused, but it does help me to forgive.

I should clarify that forgiveness is not the same as reconciliation. Neither is forgiveness a matter of forgetting what has happened. There are some hurts that preclude reconciliation—such as those of an abuser who refuses to change his behavior. Remembering those abuses actually protects us from foolish trust. Yet even the most severe wounds can be forgiven—that is, they can be released. With forgiveness, the wounded person releases his right to vindication, or revenge.

We must also learn to do more than simply forgive others. We must also forgive ourselves. As a physician, I struggle with my own inadequacy. I am often plagued with guilt about my patient care. Many disease processes are so complicated that there is little I can do to change the outcome. I find myself asking, *Did I do the right thing? Could I have recognized this illness sooner? Should I have tried another treatment first?* These thoughts have the power to hijack my peace, dragging me into the past, and throwing me into the physical consequences of the stress response. I must remember that I am human and that I—like all humans—am inadequate. I make mistakes. I need forgiveness.

Curiously, those who most struggle with *accepting* forgiveness may also struggle with *extending* forgiveness to others.

The ancient text known as The Lord's Prayer affirms this connection: "And forgive us our trespasses, as we forgive those who have trespassed against us."

Familiarity with our own weaknesses helps us to recognize ourselves in the weaknesses of others. Identifying with others helps us avoid judgment and move to understanding.

Letting go doesn't come naturally. It requires focused effort. Most of us find it easier to nurse a grudge by holding onto the offenses we suffer, sharing our frustration with anyone who will listen. However, forgiveness, this letting go, can bring a shift from resentment to peace, decreasing stress. Forgiveness is the harder road to genuine freedom, but the outcomes are totally worth it!

Anxiety. For me, anxiety or worry can be more than an emotion. It can become a negative habit that keeps me from spiritual health. It's easy to focus on the danger ahead, the what-ifs, and the unknowns ahead. Focusing on these kinds of worries robs us of the very connectedness that helps us enjoy life in the moment.

Once I had the joy of meeting a centenarian. At one hundred, alert and lively, he still played a little golf. I asked him what he thought was his secret to longevity. He answered, "I don't worry too much about things." I see a great deal of wisdom in his answer.

We humans tend to worry about two things: that which has already transpired and that which has yet to take place. Worry will never change the course of past events. Worry-filled, sleepless nights will only steal our rest. They shift us from peace to anxiety, stealing our joy. Worrying blinds us to divine encounters, deep meaning, and rewarding relationships with the people we care about most. It shifts us into the fight-or-flight response, initiating the cascade of hormones and responses that cause so much physical destruction.

Of course, it is wise to plan for the future and prepare for eventualities when we can. But we must do this from a positive emotional state. Worry is an entirely different matter. Worry is chewing endlessly on what might—but has not yet—happened and fretting over consequences that are entirely out of our control.

I fight against worry when one of my patients experiences a sudden setback. I struggle against worry when I think someone might disapprove of me or my work. I stop the churning chatter by consciously taking an emotional step backward. Giving myself a moment, I take a deep breath, becoming aware of my emotions and myself. I let these feelings come and go without judging them. When I have centered myself and calmed my body, I lift the situation up to the Divine and ask for guidance. I remind myself that I am not in control of any outcome—not my patient's and certainly not my own. In my mind, I picture myself giving this situation over to the Divine, as if I were offering someone a package.

This prayer is my way of trusting the Divine and letting go of the results. It is a way of letting my intuition participate in a vital part in my patients' care. By quieting worry, I am better able to hear from past experience, to gather wisdom from related incidents, or even to hear from the Divine. As I let go of the results, I shift back to a peaceful center—better able to do my best work, providing the best care I can—without the burden or distraction of worry.

Many people feel anxious without actually being aware of what bothers them. When worry eats away at them, they find themselves easily angered or simply irritable. Some feel vaguely pressured or unable to concentrate. Some people feel physical sensations, like a queasy stomach or tightness in the shoulders or jaw. I know one person who characterizes anxiety as a tight feeling in the chest, along with unrelenting churning in his thoughts.

If you battle with anxiety, you might begin observing yourself. Take note of your symptoms. Do you have difficulty falling asleep? Does your stomach bother you? Is it difficult to eat or to concentrate? Recognizing your own physical signs may allow you to step back and identify the cause of your anxiety. With practice, you can learn to recognize and let go of the worry and anxiety that keeps you from spiritual wellness.

Have you noticed that each of these unhealthy spiritual habits has a corresponding healthy habit? Said in its simplest form:

- **Gratitude counters complaining.**
- **Forgiveness counters resentment.**
- **Letting go overcomes anxiety.**

Wishing to live a life of wellness with my body, mind, and emotions in good health, I must not ignore my spiritual health. By establishing a daily spiritual exercise, feeding my spirit, and avoiding bad habits, I strengthen my spiritual health, just as I work toward a stronger body and growing intellect.

During my sabbatical, I put a lot of time and effort into establishing new patterns and building a new daily routine. I had already lived far too many careless years, plagued by dissatisfaction and malaise. I decided the rewards were worth the effort. My work depended on it. My life depended on it as well.

Chapter Four
STRESS

> "There is a pervasive form of contemporary violence to which the idealist most easily succumbs ... To allow oneself to be carried away by a multitude of conflicting concerns, to surrender to too many demands, to commit oneself to too many projects, to want to help everyone in everything, is to succumb to violence."
> Thomas Merton, *Conjectures of a Guilty Bystander*

Once I began to address the spiritual components of my life, I realized that I wanted to understand more about burnout. How does this syndrome progress? What is the physiological evolution of such a far-reaching disorder? What exactly had diminished me from enthusiastic, confident young doctor into lackluster, discouraged professional?

Perhaps if I understood the disease progression, I would better understand why it had happened to me. I believed my condition was related to the stress I felt at work. But was stress alone enough to cascade into burnout?

Everyone knows what stress feels like. Overcrowded freeways. Overcrowded schedules. Looming deadlines. It's the churning stomach, tight muscles, and a dead man's grip on the steering wheel. It's hurried movements, a flash of temper, and words later regretted. No doubt about it—more common than the common cold, stress has become an everyday part of our twenty-first-century life.

The American Psychological Association reported in February 2015 that 64 percent of Americans attributed their major stress to money, and 60 percent reported major work stress. In America, according to these and other reports, stress affects sleep and eating patterns, physical health, emotional satisfaction, and relationships. Depending on whom you ask, stress may contribute to such common maladies as fatigue, obesity, and heart disease.

If you are alive, you experience stress.

But what is stress exactly? What happens *inside* a person while he fights his way through the morning rush hour only to be cut off just before his exit? We can begin to understand the effects of stress by looking at balanced physiology.

Without excess stress, the human body might be viewed as a plank perfectly balanced on a pyramid. This body is rested, well fed, and well exercised. The inner physiology of the balanced body works well. Sugars are regulated. Blood pressure is normal. Weight is well maintained. A strong heart pumps in regular rhythm.

The well-balanced body responds appropriately to normal stressors—getting ready for work, climbing a set of stairs, standing from sitting, and the creative rush. When the demand for adjusted physiology wanes, the body restores its balance quickly. You might view stress as anything that interrupts that well-regulated, harmonious balance. It turns out that any number of things can throw us out of balance:

- Time pressure.
- Frustration.
- Loss (or fear of loss).
- Failure (or fear of failure).
- Compromised values.
- Imminent danger.
- Regrets.
- Life-threatening emergencies.

Stress

Any one of these might tip us from balanced physiology into stress mode. It isn't just something that happens in our heads. It happens in our bodies as well.

Our bodies react to stress or disharmony with a cascade of physiological events, including more than fourteen hundred chemical reactions and thirty different hormones. Most healthcare providers understand the physiology of the fight-or-flight response.

The sympathetic nervous system enables us to run from tigers or fight an assailant if needed. This part of the nervous system stimulates vital physical responses, increasing both heart rate and the force of each cardiac contraction. It stimulates skeletal muscles, causing increased muscle tone. It causes the adrenal glands to excrete cortisol. It increases the respiratory rate and dilates the pupils. All these responses have their function, giving us power and speed should we need them to respond to imminent danger.

The problem with these responses is that over time, with prolonged exposure to stress, they begin to cause physical harm. In fact, research has shown that prolonged exposure impairs immunity, increases blood sugar, and results in full-body inflammation.

Chronic stress has been linked to hundreds of common medical maladies. By some estimates, 75 to 90 percent of all physician visits can be attributed to stress-related complaints, including fatigue, insomnia, headaches, upset stomach, changes in appetite and sex drive, anxiety disorder, high blood pressure, depression, and skin ailments. Some who struggle with stress resort to alcohol or drug abuse as a kind of self-medication, which creates a cascade of difficulties all its own. Prolonged stress does more than tax the human body; it taxes the human soul. Even the healthiest humans living on chronic hyperdrive will eventually experience exhaustion, irritability, and impatience. Though some might describe these stress-related complaints as minor, the statistics disagree:

- Anxiety disorder increases the risk of death to four times normal.
- The angry personality is twice as likely to experience sudden death.
- Stress disorder increases the death rate by 40 percent.

Perhaps no one experiences stress more frequently than the caregiving professional involved in emergency situations. Whether in the ICU or the ER, some medical professionals in critical positions experience daily doses of extreme stress. There's nothing like a cardiac arrest to get your juices flowing. When saving lives is part of your job description, stress becomes a constant companion.

Social workers, counselors, parole officers, and teachers, many in overcrowded classrooms, also experience significant doses of daily stress. Depressed, unruly, uncooperative, or even dangerous clients, students, and parents are a part of their daily experiences. In these professions, chronic repetitive stress cannot be avoided.

These professionals might also be more susceptible to chronic stress. Those in the caring professions have big hearts. They want to help others. Generally, these overachievers are intensely competitive. They study diligently and compete for the few training positions available. Tending to see the world in an idealistic way, these professionals expect to give only the highest quality care at all times.

During their first few years on the job, they experience a heavy dose of reality. They learn that they cannot help everyone and that not everyone wants or accepts their help. Under intense time and production pressure, compromise becomes the order of the day. Some patients or clients manipulate and take advantage of care providers. Others have unreasonable expectations. Not everyone is grateful. In fact, some clients or patients reject your very best efforts to help. The work isn't easy.

As we think about stress in the workplace, I envision a simple equation that illustrates how brutal reality can create a unique kind of stress.

Stress = Expectations − Reality

Stress equals the difference between expectation and reality. This equation shows us that the quantity of stress we experience is directly related to the level of our expectations. When our experience does not meet our expectations, not only do we experience disappointment and frustration, but we may also become engaged in a struggle to change what cannot be changed. This struggle creates a stress all its own.

In the world of health care, we were trained to give the highest quality care *all the time*. As a result, we expected to help everyone who comes to us. We expected our patients to appreciate our unending effort. Instead, the realities of demanding paperwork, short staff, high patient demand, and administrative pressure keep us from regularly meeting our expectations. The result, for most of us, is stress.

A young policeman I know expresses the same disappointment. "I wanted to make a difference in my community. But it hasn't been like that. I keep going back to the same addresses, arresting the same people. The same couple keeps calling when one of them beats up on the other. The neighborhoods don't change. The people don't appreciate that I'm putting my life on the line just to defend them. It's discouraging."

While stress has the potential to keep us on our toes, helping us respond quickly and decisively in an emergency, it also has the potential to create physical and emotional havoc. Unmanaged stress, no matter where it comes from, has an emotional cost, leading to increased tension, frustration, anxiety, fear, anger, and even depression—all of which have unhealthy and sometimes life-threatening consequences. Living with a sympathetic nervous system (the fight-or-flight system) on overdrive has the potential to wear out more than the body. It can rob you of joy and serenity. If stress continues long enough, it can cause burnout. Many sources estimate that as many as one-third to one-half of all health-care providers, not just physicians, experience burnout.

At this point, our question becomes: If we want to avoid burnout, how do we manage the stress of caring for others?

Whatever answer we provide must acknowledge that some stress—such as that experienced during regular emergencies—cannot be avoided. In fact, when executing a difficult surgery, fighting a house fire, chasing bad guys, or directing a patient code, the fight-or-flight response works to our advantage.

However, after these acute stress events, the wise professional must learn how to shut down the high-alert physiology of the event, moving back into the realm of balanced calm. Anyone who has experienced this kind of intense stress reaction knows how difficult this can be. Somehow, the professional must learn to shut down the chemical and hormonal overload of the emergency as quickly as possible. We must also allow the body sufficient time to recharge when these unavoidable stressors do occur.

For most professionals, work stressors make it even more important to manage the small stressors of daily life. No one living with chronic, unrelenting stress flourishes. As we have shown, this kind of stress leads directly to illness and burnout.

So if the caregiving professional can't avoid life-threatening stressors, what can they do? The professional can learn to manage the ordinary disappointments of every day well, including time crunches, compromised care, and expectations.

This kind of stress management generally requires concerted and prolonged effort. The good news is that if you work at it, you can manage chronic, unrelenting stress. In doing so, you will experience a new joy and serenity that you might never have thought possible. I know, because I have experienced it.

Our goal, in the physiologic sense, is to shift the body from the fight-or-flight response to the relaxation response. You can picture the relaxation state by imagining yourself after a big Thanksgiving meal, calm, relaxed, and perhaps even sleepy. Your heart rate is normal; your respiration deep and regular. Your muscles and shoulders are relaxed. Your mind is quiet, without a background chatter of alarm and concern. You feel no anxiety. You can observe your own thoughts and emotions as if from a distance. You are able to concentrate without distraction or demands. You are attentive without being nervous. This relaxed state is the place where stress is least able to disrupt emotional and physiological balance.

You might ask, is this even possible? Can anyone intentionally shift from being stressed out to a more poised response? Let's begin by considering the following means of controlling the physiology of our daily experience:

MIND SHIFT

Remarkably, one of the most significant ways that we alter physiological balance involves making judgments. Whenever we label something (perhaps a circumstance or someone) as bad, we have made a mental judgment that immediately shifts the body into stress mode. The human mind does not differentiate between the judgmental declarations of bad day or bad patient and the declarations of earthquake or fire. To the mind, both events are very real. This is because the mind responds to both events by beginning the cascading hormone response that protects us in genuine emergencies. Though you may not be aware of your body's reaction, the fight-or-flight response has begun all the same.

In my experience, the first step in managing stress is to willfully shift my perceptions about the stressors in my work. While we cannot control what happens, we do have control over our own mental responses to these events. Though this takes practice, it can be done.

The Japanese writing for crisis is composed of two characters. One represents danger. The other represents critical point. These characters remind us that in any crisis, there is opportunity to redeem or improve the situation. This could be said of many of the stressful moments we experience in caring for others.

Our stressful moments do hold both danger and opportunities. When we change our thoughts about our experiences, restraining our judgments and labels, we use these critical moments to change the direction of the crisis both for our patients and ourselves. In addition, we may unearth unexpected rewards. Many of these kinds of difficult moments have taught me my most valuable lessons. Burnout is one good example.

While some would consider my experience with burnout as a long and difficult season, I now view burnout as a tremendous gift in my life. Not only did it force me to stop, consider, and change my life's course, but it has also given me the remarkable opportunity to help others rethink their own issues and stressors. The crisis of burnout held both danger (I might have given up the profession I love) and opportunity (to change myself and to help others). Burnout has given me the great joy of sharing my discoveries by speaking to audiences all over the United States—something I would never have expected. Without burnout, this book and those opportunities would not have occurred.

BREATHING

Perhaps you've heard someone say, "Take a deep breath, buddy." This advice is usually given to someone about to lose his temper. Surprisingly, this expression holds great physiological truth. The simple exercise of breathing deeply can help us begin to manage ordinary moments of stress.

By simply focusing on our breath, slowing and deepening our breathing, we shift the physiology of the body. The fight-or-flight response cannot occur concurrently with slow and relaxed breathing.

Begin by paying attention; listen to the air fill your lungs. Put your hand over your stomach and feel your stomach expand as the air flows in. Let your hand ride the expansion of your belly. Deliberately hold the air for a moment and then exhale, drawing out the exhalation for as long as possible. Repeat this exercise for about thirty seconds, shutting out all other distractions until your intense inward focus quiets your mind.

As I breathe, I imagine I am out in a stormy ocean being tossed by the waves. As I begin to pay close attention to my breathing, I feel myself sink below the tumult. In the peace below the surface, I am aware of the waves above me but am not affected by them. The screeching wind is quiet. I relax in the warm water, drifting along with the rhythm of my own breath.

To use this tool in the heat of the moment, you will need practice. I recommend that you try it at home first. In a quiet room, perhaps even on your own bed, lie down and focus on your breath. Breathe to an internal rhythm while counting through your inhalation and exhalation phases. Take longer to exhale than inhale. Doing so stimulates the vagus nerve, which mediates the parasympathetic, or relaxation, system. Doing this signals the brain to turn up the relaxation system and turn down the fight-or-flight response.

Practice this exercise at night as you drift off to sleep, and you may find you are able to fall asleep more quickly. When you are familiar with the technique, try it at work, perhaps after lunch or during a break. Eventually, you will be able to center yourself and control your breathing whenever you need to calm or quiet yourself in the midst of stress.

GRATITUDE

Scientists believe that categorizing things as bad, difficult, or overwhelming can trigger the beginning of the fight-or-flight response in the body. For instance, people respond to the idea of a classroom test in different ways. For the prepared student without test anxiety, the idea of taking a test may alert his fight-or-flight response only minimally, leaving him alert and poised, able to do his best work. He views the test positively. However, the student with many negative test experiences may immediately begin to categorize the upcoming test as difficult or alarming. These categorizations affect his body long before the test occurs, leaving him tense with rapid and shallow breathing, an elevated heart rate, physical tension, and an inability to concentrate. Making negative declarations about upcoming events can contribute to creating a more difficult reality.

By cultivating gratitude in the face of difficulty, we can shift the body's response from fight-or-flight to relaxation. I have found this simple gratitude behavior to be hugely powerful in changing my response. While this technique may seem insignificant, you must experience it to understand its power.

Most of us tend to complain and grumble more than we think. If it is true that negative evaluations and complaints trigger the sympathetic nervous system, then most of us experience an onslaught of fight-or-flight hormones many times daily. It's no wonder depression, anxiety, high blood pressure, and high blood sugar are so rampant.

You may think that you are different and that you don't complain that much. I did too—until I faced my own reality. You already know how that went. I knew immediately that I'd need to make real changes. I decided that my first step in combating these negative thoughts would be to keep a gratitude journal. Every night, I took a moment and wrote down three or four things for which I was grateful. As you know, at first I wrote down the glaringly obvious:

I have a job.
I get paid.
I have a roof over my head.

My early efforts weren't very inspired. But as I persisted, the list became more personal and more meaningful. I discovered that my gratitude began to evolve, opening my eyes to the many good things I experienced every day. Over time, I realized that I had to do more than make a list. I needed to turn this constant habit of grumbling and complaining into a habit of gratitude. Instead of waiting to write in my journal, I wanted gratitude to invade my day during the moments when I experienced stress.

That was a little more difficult. In the beginning, I remember that my gratitude felt entirely forced—even a little absurd. For example, I remember once looking at my afternoon schedule and realizing that one of my most difficult patients was scheduled for two o'clock that afternoon. Mrs. Jones, as I'll call her, always demanded more time and better results than I could provide. On an ordinary day, I might have spent the morning dreading her arrival. On that particular day, determined to be grateful for something, the best I could do was to utter, "At least the whole afternoon isn't filled with Mrs. Jones."

It wasn't much, but it represented a small beginning. Over time, I began to be grateful for patients like Mrs. Jones for more personal reasons. These patients helped me grow my listening skills and my compassion. Through them, I learned to be fully present, even with difficult people. As I grew in gratitude, my dread of these kinds of patients eased.

Gradually, I replaced the habit of complaining with the habit of gratitude. In the process, I realized that anything you complain about could be viewed from a grateful perspective. I could choose to view my alarm clock as a reminder that I'd been given another day to live. The rain reminded me of the beauty of the rich, green landscape of the Pacific Northwest. Even when my morning shower turned cold, I was grateful that my sometimes slow moving son was up to begin his day—without any prodding from me.

I discovered that no matter what I was dealing with, I could find a way to be grateful. Learning to look for gratitude eased my stress. Remarkably, both my scientific understanding of stress and my spiritual exploration of wellness were pointing me in the same direction.

I needed to learn to forgive, to let go, and to be grateful.

These early steps opened doors with benefits I had not imagined.

Though I could not eliminate all stress from my work, I began to deal with daily stressors by choosing a response that shut down or minimized the fight-or-flight response. Remarkably, my days became more bearable. Still, I knew I had much more to learn.

Chapter Five
EXPLORING AUTHENTIC SPIRITUALITY

> "How glorious the splendor of a human
> heart that trusts that it is loved!"
> Brennan Manning, author and speaker

The more I thought about stress and burnout, the more science and spirituality seemed to support and verify one another, braiding principles together that, in a surprising way, reinforce one another. Science tells me that living in a constant state of fight-or-flight damages my body. Spirituality tells me that living in this stress-filled and anxious state damages my soul. Science and spirituality agree that taking control of how I live involves changing the way I respond to stress.

At this point, you might be thinking, "This is getting too religious for me." I understand your concern. As discussed earlier, for many, the experience of religion has not helped them feel more connected to the Divine or others. Religion often takes advantage of others, controlling people and populations via manipulation and fear, and can separate us from the Divine through guilt.

Spirituality is a different animal entirely. I'd like to show you how.

Spirituality is a broad concept with room for many perspectives. One can say however, that it includes a sense of connection to something bigger than ourselves, and it typically involves a search for meaning in life. The spiritual world is mysterious. In fact, the Lakota people use a word for God, *Wakan Tanka*, that is sometimes translated "Great Spirit." I am told that it is more accurately translated "Great Mystery." Great Mystery may be a good word for the Divine because spirituality demands humility and openness to things we cannot see.

So, how might we recognize authentic spirituality? In order for spirituality to impact us or make a difference in the world, it must be genuine. It must exist beneath the surface of our language and behavior; it must be forceful enough to shape our life choices. We have already said that spirituality is more than dogma—more than rules and regulations. But what does authentic spirituality really look like? What qualities do you find in the life of someone with authentic spirituality? Let me attempt to describe someone who lives in authentic spirituality:

1. Trust. The person with authentic spirituality displays a steadfast trust—a belief that someone or something out there is in control and that this Divine entity is characterized by loving goodness. He or she believes that the Divine genuinely cares for us. They exhibit trust in their ability to let go of outcomes—even tremendously important ones. Trust keeps the spiritual person from being reactive to people and circumstances. Instead, because the spiritual person has let go of his or her stake in the game, he or she accepts detours, bumps, and dead ends without losing his or her sense of safety and security. In trust, the spiritual person makes well-considered decisions and choices, even in the face of adversity.

There is a Zen tradition about trust and letting go. It goes something like this:

> *Let go a little, and you have a little peace.*
> *Let go a lot, and you have a lot of peace.*
> *Let go completely, and you have complete peace.*

The authentically spiritual person is able to let go of the desire for things to be different. This doesn't mean that he or she doesn't take responsibility or try to effectively change what can be changed. Perhaps the most important motivator of this letting go is growing confidence and trust in divine love. On the deepest spiritual level, the universal language of humanity is love. Love holds all things together. Why wouldn't the Divine be love personified?

Joan Borysenko, a pioneer in the area integrative medicine and the mind-body connection, clarifies this idea. According to Borysenko, we are all in the hands of a loving force, and all our experiences in life are meant by that loving force to lead us into greater freedom.

For many, the idea of trusting a mysterious divine power can be clouded by a painful religious history, perhaps one dominated by rigid rules, severe discipline, and fear. Perhaps we experienced difficult childhood experiences with authority figures who were cruel, unloving, or inattentive. These memories can inhibit our ability to even consider the possibility of divine love. Backgrounds like these might actually lead us toward religion rather than toward the authentically spiritual life.

2. Connection. It is not enough to simply acknowledge the Divine. Persons with authentic spirituality are deeply connected with the Divine. For these people, the Divine is not some unknowable, untouchable, uninterested force out there. Instead, the Divine is personal, interested, caring, and purposeful.

Authentic spirituality seeks to establish and maintain a meaningful connection with the Divine. This connection with the Divine motivates and enables the spiritual person to approach others from a position of loving-kindness. It empowers and emboldens the authentically spiritual to exhibit these same divine qualities toward the rest of humanity.

George Vaillant, psychiatrist and professor of medicine at Harvard, believes that humans are hardwired for spirituality. He bases his entire definition of spirituality on this one factor—connectedness. According to Vaillant, this connection is manifested by emotions such as awe, gratitude, love, compassion, and forgiveness. In the authentically spiritual life, connection to the Divine is valued and nurtured.

Those who are authentically spiritual have learned to deepen their connection with the Divine. Though we may feel separated from the Divine, unworthy, perhaps even doubting the nature of such a love, the authentically spiritual fight through doubt. They create space and habits that develop trust and connection. Some find this connection in the miracle of nature. Others in stillness and quiet. Still others in the words of inspirational writing. With deliberate focus, spiritually authentic people nurture a connection with the Divine.

3. Compassion. Compassion flows from connection to the Divine. One rarely happens without the other. Authentic spirituality is not content with connection to the Divine. Instead, authentic spirituality expresses itself in compassion toward the rest of the world. More than warm feelings toward humanity, compassion moves the authentically spiritual person toward actions that benefit humanity—in large and small ways. Compassion driven by authentic spirituality connects us both to one another and to our communities. Eventually, it connects us to our world.

As we grow our relationship and connection with the Divine, we grow in divine love, eventually becoming secure enough in this love to share it with others. The greater our connection with the Divine, the stronger our faith or trust. As we become secure in that love, we give ourselves and our possessions away without fear of loss.

Fred Buechner, author of Wishful Thinking: A Theological ABC, says, "The place God calls you to is the place where your deep gladness and the world's deep hunger meet." Those who are authentically spiritual gain energy and satisfaction at this intersection of giftedness and need. Through their connection with the Divine, they receive their calling, sharing their gift in any way they can.

4. **Divine guidance.** The authentically spiritual believe that the Divine uses humans to accomplish important things. Because of this, the authentically spiritual see their work as the Divine's compassionate and loving gift to humanity. Believing this, those who are authentically spiritual are not afraid to seek divine guidance wherever they need it. Getting quiet, these people open themselves to experience the mystery of the inner life. They establish a connection with the Divine and boldly ask for guidance. They are not surprised to discover unexpected answers to their questions.

This gift, the remarkable and perfectly timed appearance of creative solutions, unusual approaches, or unusual direction, may be the greatest benefit of living the authentically spiritual life. These surprising solutions can be energizing, giving the authentically spiritual energy and endurance.

But these people do more than ask for guidance. Expecting to receive direction, the authentically spiritual also respond to the wisdom they receive. They are not afraid to try the new ideas that seem to come from this guidance. Over time, as they become more experienced with divine guidance, seeking to live in harmony with the divine love of the universe, they experience less fear, more trust, and greater joy.

5. **Peace.** Authentically spiritual people live at peace with others and with themselves. This is not to say that they enjoy everyone or that they don't experience conflict. But the authentically spiritual person recognizes a key truth about others, which is based on his own understanding of himself. As he is loved, others are also loved. Others have value. Others make mistakes. Others are also on journeys toward becoming their best selves.

Because of this understanding, the authentically spiritual can overlook the offenses of others, letting go of the injuries and wounds inflicted by others. Unwilling to live at the mercy of their own reactions and grudges, authentically spiritual people work toward forgiving others. They avoid adversarial relationships and retaliation.

Authentically spiritual people also experience a unique peace that gives them stability in the face of offenses, surprises, and frustrations. This peace protects them from reactivity. At the same time, this inner peace enables them to maintain their connection with the Divine, seeking guidance and power to follow through on whatever guidance they may receive—even in the face of severe conflict or crisis.

In a world of filled with dogma, religion, and war, a world driven by the fight for religious dominance, authentic spirituality is a rare thing. Though it is free to all, authentic spirituality is the possession of few.

As I learned from the Medicine Man, my lack of authentic spirituality left me dry, frustrated, and deeply unhappy. In this condition, we humans are less likely to share our gifts with the world and more likely to express our bitterness, resentment, and disappointment.

Speaking practically, how does authentic spirituality impact our daily lives? Is it about church attendance? Ceremony? Not really. A short time ago, I experienced a situation that would have demolished me during my season of burnout. Instead, in a season of burgeoning spirituality, I experienced something quite different.

Every year, our teaching staff spends months searching for ideal candidates for our family practice residency program. They read applications, selected, and interviewed candidates and finally chose our candidates for the match.

Through the match system, medical school graduates select and prioritize their desired programs for post-medical-school training. At the same time, institutions prioritize their favorite students. Then, using an algorithm, a computer matches new doctors and institutions. However, one year, in spite of all our work, we were awarded only three matches for the four positions we had available. Demoralized and embarrassed, our staff felt frustrated that we hadn't secured the candidates who would best fit our program.

At work, the mood was gloomy. I found it hard not to give in to group depression. However, I made a conscious decision to let go of the things I felt and the things that seemed wrong, placing my faith in our mission and purpose, while at the same time trusting that the Divine had a bigger purpose for this unusual event.

Somehow, I felt the Divine would bring the right person to us.

Not long after, we were contacted by a young man who had not been matched with his chosen institutions. Though he had applied to emergency medicine programs, his second choice was family practice. When his application arrived, I marveled at his qualifications. He should have matched easily. What glitch in the system had kept him from being placed? I called him for a telephone interview and later met with him in person. I was surprised to meet an outstanding candidate whom I invited to join our program.

This young man became one of our most outstanding residents. Every time I think of him, I smile. This deeply frustrating situation led us to a candidate more qualified than any we had chosen on our own. I like to say we "traded up"! Through connection with the Divine, I asked for and received unexpected guidance. Trusting that the Divine had a better plan, we experienced the joy of training this remarkable physician.

Chapter Six
THE BENEFITS OF A HEALTHY SPIRITUAL LIFE

"Stress can destroy so much more than our physical health. Too often it eats away at our hope, belief and faith."
Dr. Charles Glassman, author of *Brain Drain*

In the process of climbing out of my emotional hole, I had to face the truth. Neglecting my spiritual life had limited my ability to manage my own stress. I hadn't considered how an empty spiritual life played into my condition and how the constant flow of stress hormones had taken its toll. It's no wonder I was exhausted. When I considered my situation in the context of human physiology, it made sense. As I looked around, observing others who successfully coped with a stress-filled life, I began to recognize the benefits of a balanced life.

Those who somehow manage to keep a life-work-spirit balance experience the world quite differently. Not only do they avoid burnout, but their lives exhibit advantages I had only dreamed about. The more I studied, the more rewards I uncovered.

Not only do these spiritual benefits directly affect our work lives, living a life with authentic spirituality brings benefits to family and mentoring relationships, as well as interactions and relationships with the broader community. In the context of burnout, you'll discover that one of the most critical of these benefits includes recovering the passion and energy you once experienced in your professional life.

ADVANTAGES OF HEALTHY SPIRITUALITY

Though doing so requires commitment, I have found that growing a healthy spiritual life provides four distinct advantages:

1. A sense of calling. Those with a strong spiritual life sense a divine call in their work. Their employment situation is more than just a job. They believe that something bigger and more important than money or position has brought them to their work. They are convinced that this divine force seeks to act both *in* and *through* them. This sense of calling adds both meaning and purpose to their work.

When we feel called to our work, we view daily interactions from the perspective of divine appointments rather than drudgery. This divine call helps us view our present position (*where* we serve) as purposeful rather than accidental. When we have a sense of calling, we understand that *who we are*—our unique giftedness and personhood—is a divine gift to our workplace. At the same time, we understand and appreciate that the workplace provides us with unique opportunities and gifts sent to us from the Divine. We are a gift to our workplaces, and our workplaces are a gift to us.

This viewpoint changes our perspective about the circumstances that brought us to our current positions. Rather than see our placements as a random combination of interactions and open doors, we view them through the perspective of divine placement.

I have learned to view my own work environment in this way. As I prepared for a career in medicine, I had hoped to work in a third-world country, providing care to underserved populations. When I finished my training, the organizations I most respected were not placing families abroad. Because I already had three children, they would not hire me. I was forced to seek other employment.

During my residency, I'd volunteered in a small Native American clinic in Wichita, Kansas. Because I'd had a good experience there, someone suggested I attend the Indian Health Service Recruitment Conference. I went hoping to find an open position in the Pacific Northwest, near my wife's family. Unfortunately, the Indian Health Service had no openings there.

After the meeting, while waiting for an elevator, a stranger asked me if I'd found a position. I admitted that I hadn't and explained my situation. The stranger commented, "You should check with the Puyallup Tribe. I hear they're looking for a doctor."

The Puyallup Tribe had just begun managing its own health clinic, and for this reason, their openings had not been included in any of the IHS information I'd received. I pursued this new information—information provided by a complete stranger in an apparently accidental meeting—eventually landing my first job in Tacoma, Washington, smack in the middle of the Pacific Northwest.

Without that "chance" meeting at the elevators, I would have never found my current position. Viewed from a spiritual perspective, that chance interaction becomes direction from the Divine. This viewpoint helps me see my work as more than a job; it helps me to recognize that I have been sent, appointed by the Divine, to serve in this unique community. Because of my distinct set of gifts, or perhaps because of the things I am to gain in this setting, I feel called to work for the Puyallup Tribe. Though I may not always understand how my gifting fits, or what great benefit I derive from my work, my spiritual life allows me to trust this divine call.

This sense of calling has profound implications when my work gets tough and when my circumstances become intensely difficult. Believing that I've been called gives me extra energy and deeper resolve in the midst of stressful situations. It expands my viewpoint and forces me to consider the bigger picture, as well as the needs of others. My divine call reminds me that my work is about more than my own reward and satisfaction. With this point of view, I recognize that my work is also about growth, meaning, development, gifts, and, most importantly, service. When things are at their worst, this viewpoint allows me to move beyond my own discomfort and look for deeper meanings and unseen potential. The concept of calling leads to the second benefit of a spiritual perspective.

2. Improved attitude. In an often-quoted poem, Chuck Swindoll, author and speaker, writes about the importance of attitude:

> The longer I live, the more I realize the importance of choosing the right attitude in life. Attitude is more important than facts. It is more important than your past; more important than your education or your financial situation; ...
>
> Life is like a violin. You can focus on the broken strings that dangle, or you can play your life's melody on the one string that remains ... your attitude.

Your attitude determines how you interpret the things that happen both *to* you and *around* you. Whether you are aware of it or not, your attitude determines the ways you speak to yourself about those things. In an oft-cited Stanford Research Institute report on work success, attitude was determined to be the most important variable in predicting success, even more important than giftedness. In fact, 88 percent of success was attributed entirely to attitude.

Can we intentionally change our attitude? Can we alter deeply entrenched thoughts, feelings, and beliefs? Or are we simply stuck with the attitudes we hold—whether they came from our genetic make-up, modeling, training, or hard knocks?

I believe that we do have the ability to change our attitude, though this is not easy. By changing our attitude, we will change the level of satisfaction we derive from our daily experiences—including those at work. This ability to change our attitude is enhanced by growing the spiritual aspect of our lives.

As we continue to feed our spirits, we experience a subtle but significant change. We become aware of the inherent opportunities in our work. Awake to the Divine, we carry a sense of expectancy rather than defensiveness. We live with the wonder of possibility, aware of the Divine's presence. We anticipate that divine guidance will arrive just when we most need it. No longer driven by anxiety, fear of loss or failure, we are empowered to abandon our defensive position.

Cultivating my spiritual health, I now recognize each day as its own gift. I lean forward with potential wonder toward each moment, each interaction, and each experience. Spiritual health doesn't turn us into Pollyanna people, expecting success at every turn. It doesn't deny our real frustrations either. Rather, spiritual health turns us into people of anticipation—people who approach their days and their duties while staying open to each surprising turn of events that might occur during any ordinary day. This positive attitude leads us to the next benefit of a strong spiritual life.

3. Transformed expectations. As we've already shown, stress occurs when what we experience falls short of our expectations. Whether your experience involves a disappointing room at an expensive resort or an ideal job applicant who becomes a second-rate employee, the difference between what you expect and what you experience can leave you feeling frustrated and stressed.

And the bigger the difference between your expectations and your experience, the more overwhelming the stress you feel. I admit that when I took my first job, I naively expected to help all my patients. I believed that all my patients would love and appreciate me. Of course, neither of these unrealistic expectations were met. With such lofty ideals, you can imagine how intensely frustrated I felt about my clinical experience.

This difference—between our expectations and our experiences—is perhaps more strongly felt here in the United States, where our culture focuses on the smallest disappointments. If we have nine things go right in our day, we obsess over the one thing that went wrong. Though I cannot prove it, I believe this tends not to be a problem in less prosperous cultures. In those places, I have observed populations who stop to celebrate the one thing in ten that goes well!

A person with a strong spiritual life—one who senses a divine call and who has a good attitude about his work—is less likely to be hobbled by unreasonable or unrealistic expectations. That person is less likely to be attached to specific, personal agendas. Instead, he or she meets the day with an open heart and open spirit, welcoming surprising—even difficult—diversions as manifestations of the Divine.

This does not mean that we lower our standards of care. It does not mean that, for the sake of convenience, we stop seeking excellence. Rather, it means that we view interruptions, inconveniences, and surprises as part of the Divine's purpose for the day. Let me share a personal illustration.

One day at our clinic, long before the dawn of electronic records, it came to my attention that one of our patients had been left in an exam room for some time. Investigating the situation, I discovered that the provider involved was waiting for the patient's paper medical chart. From long experience, I knew the chart could be anywhere; our clinic is a large and busy place, providing medical, dental, pharmacy, social, and psychological services. In spite of a lengthy search, no one could locate the chart. Without it, our provider refused to see the patient.

I understood this doctor's frustration. Normally, I expect to have a paper chart in hand when I met with a patient, to maintain accuracy, follow up on issues, and provide quality care. But in this particular case, this normal expectation had interrupted the flow of the entire clinic, creating a great inconvenience for the patient.

I found the provider pouting at his desk and gently suggested that for this one visit we might consider this absent chart a potential gift. Because a chart tends to keep us focused on a narrow list of complaints and issues, perhaps this no-chart visit might lead to some new understanding, clearer health goals, or perhaps a clarification of the current complaint.

Because the provider was strongly connected to a narrow agenda of procedures and expectations—that he saw patients only with a chart in hand—he had already experienced extreme frustration. His anger and attitude kept him from bringing his best gifts to his work. His frustration had interrupted care for an entire clinic, causing suffering for many people. Yet my growing spiritual awareness led me to view the situation as an opportunity rather than a frustration.

As I shared that idea with my staff member, the physician reluctantly agreed to see the chartless patient. And indeed, the less structured visit opened up an unexpected area of discussion on a deeper level with the patient, resulting in a very beneficial interaction.

I now approach my workday with expectancy rather than expectations. By trusting the Divine, I am open to the good that may come from unexpected complications or circumstances that arise in an otherwise ordinary day.

4. Ability to let go. It is especially easy for highly trained, highly motivated, and highly competitive people to develop control issues. For the most part, we have learned that by eliminating as much risk or hazard as possible, we experience better results—whether these include better patient outcomes, fewer injuries for firefighters or policemen, or better test results for students and school districts.

This drive explains the demanding dentist who must have every treatment tray perfectly set up and his tools presented in precise order. It accounts for the surgeon who must control every detail of the surgical suite (including music and temperature), according to his own tight specifications. I knew of one receptionist who couldn't work without her pens and pencils lined up in a specific order on her desk. Heaven help the employee who borrowed her writing utensils.

The danger comes when we believe that by controlling every variable in our environments, we can eliminate anything from interfering with our goals.

A strong spiritual life frees us from the overwhelming need to manage everything in our environments. As we become aware of the Divine, we recognize that we control very little beyond the small items in our sphere of influence. The heart of the spiritual life is mystery. As we grow our spiritual lives, we are better able to let go of those things that we cannot control. Trust lies at the heart of the spiritual life.

As I've explained, trust is openness to the Divine's will. It is the ability to accept outcomes that do not line up with our own. All great spirituality is essentially about letting go, not about trusting in our own rites, rituals, and habits. Great spirituality is the ability to trust something much bigger, much wiser, and much more powerful than our private management strategies.

Letting go of our need to control requires that we recognize those situations, people, and outcomes we cannot change and acknowledge our circumstances for what they are. While sometimes these situations are unwanted, or even devastating, letting go of control helps us move beyond our own emotions and our own tight-fisted wish for things to be different. As we let go, we move into a place where we can receive guidance about what to do next. By accepting what *is* in this matter-of-fact way, we begin to move forward to what *could* be.

So far, we've been discussing the advantages of growing our spiritual lives. In a broad sense, building a strong spiritual foundation helps us to experience four advantages: a sense of calling, an improved attitude, transformed expectations, and the ability to let go.

GIFTS OF SPIRITUAL HEALTH

But there is more. If we are willing to dive more deeply into spiritual wellness, these simple advantages will transform themselves into gifts—treasured, life-giving, world-changing gifts. These gifts help us face the pressure of a difficult workplace without succumbing to the mind-numbing frustration that leads to burnout. When you live within the blessing of these gifts, you will discover both a new anchor and a new freedom.

1. Purpose. If we accept that the Divine has called us to our work (divine calling), it follows naturally that the Divine desires to accomplish something vital through our work. This is especially important when we consider our work in the context of people. The most sacred element of our work, the element most crucial to our divine calling, involves helping people. This is our divine purpose.

This life-changing viewpoint tells us that we are more than salary earners. We are more than production goals. We are more than statistics. We serve the Divine by helping people. As you experience this gift, you might even begin to consider your work holy—whether you teach children, keep people safe, battle fires, or fight physical illness. As your spiritual life deepens, you will begin to see that you actually represent the Divine as you help people through difficult circumstances.

2. Presence. If you accept that you are an agent of the Divine, destined to serve people, then it follows naturally that the Divine will desire to help you in your work. This is no surprise. Those who serve in the Red Cross expect the organization to provide the needed provisions in order to complete their work. In the same way, if your work is divine work, then you can expect the Divine wants to respond when you ask for divine guidance or provision. As we uncover the meaning of this great gift—of divine presence, support, and provision—we unearth resources bigger than our own and understanding deeper than our training. Divine presence allows us to step beyond our own instincts, abilities, or preparations.

By inviting the Divine into our work, we access an unending well of provision. This is not to say that we expect the Divine to immediately download dramatic cures for cancer or provide the lesson plans for your next class. Instead, we live in daily expectation of divine insight, each piece revealed to us at exactly the right moment.

Sometimes, the Divine reveals a problem to me that I have not yet recognized or allows me to link problems with issues I might not have otherwise connected. The Divine may lead me to information sources I had not previously considered. These gifts are indications of the Divine's presence in my work. Not only do they help me to solve difficult problems, but they help me feel less isolated, overwhelmed, or lost.

In order to appreciate the twin gifts of divine purpose and divine presence, we must become more fully present and aware as we work, alert for these remarkable answers to our requests. Living this way reveals new resources to help those we serve.

Living in expectancy, we step back from the chaos, conflict, and politics of our work. Fully aware of the Divine, we are no longer driven to win, to accomplish, to achieve, or to accumulate. Instead, we are free to be simply and fully present. We experience work moments free of demands, drives, implications, and agendas. Because the Divine has called us, has given us purpose, and is with us, we are able to rest in the moment, knowing that something bigger than ourselves has each situation in hand.

3. Spiritual power. As we embrace our spirituality, along with our divine call to our work, we begin to experience the Divine's presence helping us accomplish our tasks. This will soon lead us to discover the unexpected gift of spiritual power. No longer emotionally subject to the whims of circumstances, frustrations, or conflict, we have the remarkable power to choose calmness and peace.

This third gift of spiritual power springs from the first two. When we accept the gifts of divine purpose and presence, we can finally let go of our need to control outcomes and manipulate people. Spiritual power equates to trusting the Divine as we begin to recognize our own lack of control in the world. We accept that we cannot direct other people's behaviors, decisions, responses, or interactions. Trust allows us to stop trying.

In the workplace, trust enables us to believe that divine purpose and presence will take us through difficult or demanding situations. In even the most trying conditions, trust believes that we may expect to find surprising but important answers in our work—in spite of others. This kind of trust doesn't come easily. With practice, as we feed our spirits and grow spiritually, as we work on our responses, this gift of power manifests itself.

> Antoine de Saint-Exupéry says in his novella *The Little Prince*,
> "And now here is my secret, a very simple secret:
> It is only with the heart that one can see rightly;
> what is essential is invisible to the eye."

This is the point of the third gift. As we accept our divine purpose and recognize the divine presence, we recognize that we have great power to shape the course of our own happiness. While we have no control over others, we can have complete control of our own inner world.

Though you cannot necessarily see, touch, or measure it, the health of our inner worlds colors everything about our daily satisfaction, peace, and happiness. When you exercise your spiritual power the inner world cannot be touched by the things that happen to us. It cannot be broken by the thoughtlessness or cruelty of others. Because it belongs to us alone, we have complete control and responsibility for what we allow to dwell in our inner world. We can surrender to our own unhappy thoughts, complaints, and dissatisfactions, or we can choose to dwell in gratitude, self-awareness, and trust.

This third gift, the gift of spiritual power, reminds us that our well-being is determined not by our circumstances but by the condition of our inner world, a condition which we have the ability to control.

This is similar to a principle I first learned in high school biology. Stimulus-response theory proposes that behavior is learned, predictable, and altered by paired conditioning.

You may remember the formula as:

$$S \rightarrow R.$$

Stimulus leads to response.

Applying this formula to daily life might look like this: Being cut off on the freeway stimulates an angry response. Being passed over for a promotion stimulates a resentful response. The idea is that our responses are dictated by the stimuli we experience. Contemporary marketing wants us to believe these kinds of lies. If I had a Lexus, I'd be happy. If a woman wears this perfume, she will attract this kind of man. Some of us may use this very formula to unwittingly abdicate personal responsibility, saying things like, "I only lost my temper because she didn't get that document to me on time."

However, when it comes to personal happiness, it turns out that a specific stimulus does not have to produce a specific response. Modern research supports this idea—that the bulk of responsibility for our own happiness resides *within* us. Current psychological theory states that most people have a predetermined level of happiness. Though circumstances—like buying a new car—may alter our sense of happiness for a short period, most people soon return to their previous level of happiness. This idea is referred to as the happiness set point. This is similar to the phrase "hedonistic habituation," coined by scientists Kennon M. Sheldon and Sonja Lyubomirsy in 2007. They concluded the human mind gets used to a particular experience, no matter how highly anticipated that experience might have been.

I observed this myself recently in a patient who had won our state's lotto. Prior to winning, he was chronically unhappy, his daily conversation characterized by worry and complaint. I saw him in the clinic about a year after his big win. I expected his financial gains might have eliminated his negative outlook. To my surprise, his eight-figure win hadn't changed him in the least.

"It's not all that great," he told me. "You can't find safe financial advisers. I'm not sure what to do with it all. People call all the time asking for money."

He'd quickly habituated to his new financial status and returned to his chronic patterns of worry and complaint.

Though no one is certain, scientists believe that genetics may account for as much as half of our happiness set point; the rest may be altered by our attitudes and thought lives.

Research also affirms the effects of gratitude on happiness. According to an Eastern Washington University study, the grateful person tends to be a happier person. This idea is not new; Abraham Lincoln said something similar almost 150 years ago: "Folks are usually as happy as they make up their minds to be."

When we abdicate our responsibility for our own happiness, we live by that old biological stimulus-response theory, which reduces us to nothing more than single-celled plankton, unable to think, interpret, or choose actions for ourselves. Instead of that formula, I prefer to put a delta signal above the arrow, like this:

$$S \xrightarrow{\Delta} R$$

The Benefits of a Healthy Spiritual Life

The delta sign is used in science to indicate a catalyst or change agent. I use it here to represent that our responses are determined not just by the stimuli we experience, but also by our interpretations of the events, by our attitudes about the events, by the people involved in the events, and by the spiritual meanings we discern in the midst of the circumstance.

Our responses are shaped not just by what happens to us, but also by the ways that we interpret what has happened.

Viktor Frankl, an Austrian neurologist and psychiatrist, said something similar. As a holocaust survivor who experienced unimaginable cruelty while imprisoned in three different concentration camps, he wrote in *Man's Search for Meaning*, "Everything can be taken from a man but one thing: the last of human freedoms—to choose one's attitude in any given set of circumstances, to choose one's own way."

When we accept the gifts of divine purpose and divine presence, we expand our repertoire of interpretations, enabling us to view our difficult experiences in more meaningful and satisfying ways. Our interpretations shape our responses to the things we experience. Consider this story, shared in the book *Kitchen Table Wisdom* by physician Rachel Naomi Remen: Great Italian psychiatrist Roberto Assagioli wrote a parable about interviewing three stonecutters all building a fourteenth-century cathedral. In the story, the interviewer asks each worker, "What are you doing?"

The first explains that he is cutting stone into blocks. He then describes in frustration that this is something he has done over and over and will repeat until he dies.

The second stonecutter—who is assigned to the same task—replies with warmth. He is providing food and clothing for his children and shelter for his beloved family.

The third stonecutter responds with joy. He is proud to build this glorious cathedral, which will stand as a lighthouse for humanity for thousands of years.

Each of the three men, doing exactly the same job, interprets his work in a vastly different way. This famous parable leads us to the question: Does the interpretation of their work *reflect* how the stonecutters feel? Or does the interpretation *shape* how they feel? Most theorists believe that our interpretations of the world directly influence how we feel about our lives, our work, and ourselves. In the case of these stonecutters, their interpretations of their work might even impact the duty and excellence with which they complete that work. Though each has the same skill and is completing the same task, because of their unique viewpoints each worker experiences vastly different levels of personal satisfaction.

We too can alter our personal satisfaction and happiness when we take control of our inner lives, accepting the gifts of purpose, presence, and power.

Chapter Seven
MINDFULNESS

> "The miracle of love comes to you in the presence of the uninterrupted moment. If you are mentally somewhere else, you miss real life."
> Byron Katie, speaker and author of *A Thousand Names for Joy*

The transition from my grumbling, complaining mindset into a pattern of gratitude required time and practice. As you know, I began by keeping a gratitude journal, sitting down every evening to write down the things for which I was grateful. This proved tremendously helpful in shifting my focus. I knew that I wanted to live predominantly under the control of what physiologists call my parasympathetic nervous system— the rest-and-digest state of mind—rather than in the stress-filled, anxiety-driven world of fight-or-flight. I called my goal, this rested, relaxed state, *resonance*.

It wasn't easy to make this shift. Gratitude helped me change my outlook on the bumps in my professional life. But gratitude alone wouldn't protect me from the adrenaline surge I experienced when I faced unhappy patients or conflicts among my coworkers. I needed something more. It was then that I discovered a skill that helped me reach resonance called mindfulness.

Until recently, the idea of mindfulness—the exercise of being fully present in the moment—was uncharted territory, pursued only by mystics and monks. At the time I encountered the practice, it was a relatively new concept. Of the scores of mindfulness studies now available, only a few were published before 2005.

These days, mindfulness has almost become a fad, attracting researchers of all kinds. Experts are currently exploring mindfulness as it relates to the health sciences, psychology, business, music, and competitive sports. No matter which expert you consult, there is no doubt that mindfulness has tremendous potential.

In 2014 more than two thousand employees from Google, Facebook, and Instagram participated in a single mindfulness conference called Wisdom 2.0. The program was deemed a tremendous success, so much so that today, along with health care, health clubs, and other perks, Google offers its 52,000 employees free classes in mindfulness. With the aim of increasing employee productivity and satisfaction, Google has heavily invested in the mindfulness phenomenon.

There is ample evidence that practicing meditative mindfulness has significant benefits. In a study published in the May 2014 *Journal of Psychological Science*, researchers found that when undergraduate students practiced ten minutes of daily mindfulness, they measurably increased their memory's working capacity along with their ability to maintain focused attention.

Mindfulness need not be confined to meditative practices. Mindfulness can also be a valuable tool when used in the midst of the most stressful parts of a hectic day. In my case, I consider mindfulness to be the practice of being fully present in the moment, relaxed, and undistracted by judgment or attachment. In mindfulness, I do not evaluate the situation as bad or good. I do not label people or problems. I reject my drive to control outcomes. Using mindfulness, I seek to be completely focused yet composed, balanced, and level-headed. By practicing mindfulness in the midst of difficult events, I shift myself from alarm, anxiety, frustration, and even anger (classic conditions of the fight-or-flight state) to a calm, highly aware condition where I perform my best.

For me, mindfulness was more than a revelation. It was a gift.

Mindfulness

I remember one particular day when I became convinced of the power of this gift. During that afternoon, I had a very full patient schedule when a problem developed at the hospital. An issue with a patient in labor needed attention. At the same time, I was still mulling over a difficult quandary with the health board. Normally, I like to resolve issues before I move on to patient care. But none of these issues had been resolved. Before I began my mindfulness practice, I would have tried to treat patients with my mind elsewhere, full of worry, conflict, and uncertainty. On any ordinary day, this distraction would have kept me from listening to my patients, and the resulting miscommunication would have complicated patient care, amplifying my frustration.

On that afternoon, I practiced mindfulness before starting my appointment schedule. At the end of the day, I was surprised by the peace and efficiency I'd felt while caring for my patients. That day, the gift of mindfulness was a revelation. I've learned that if I pause in the midst of the everyday tumult to focus on my own breath, I become more aware of myself. In this place, I observe my circumstances and emotions as if from a distance. I become aware of my body—of the sensations I experience, like shoulder tension and a clenching jaw. As I step back mentally, I feel a heightened awareness of my environment—of the room, the light, and the people around me. In the process of mindfulness, aware of myself in the context of the here and now, it is almost as if I become hyper alive in some strange way. The practice creates a space where I identify with my observant self, not with my reactive self. I am fully present and highly focused. I am aware, poised, and ready to engage with my best self, rather than my stressed out self.

In practicing mindfulness one attempts to let go of judgment. While I acknowledge that part of me might be feeling anger or anxiety, mindfulness allows me to be aware of difficult feelings without identifying myself as the feeling itself. Rather than declaring, "I am angry," mindfulness allows me simply to be aware of the *feeling* of anger. This is not unlike how a scuba diver sitting on the sea floor might be aware of the heavy wave action at the ocean's surface—aware, but unaffected. Mindfulness is characterized by this kind of detachment—aware, though separate from the events and emotions around you.

What do I mean when I say that mindfulness avoids judgment? Outside of mindfulness, we might conclude, "This is a terrible situation," or, "He has ruined everything," even before an experience is over. Mindfulness keeps us from reaching these conclusions, allowing us to recognize the potential in any given moment. Mindfulness recognizes that a difficult beginning might lead us toward a wonderful result.

I have heard an old proverb that illustrates this principle:

In a very small village lived a farmer with a prized horse. One day the horse ran away. The villagers came to sympathize with the farmer, saying, "This is terrible luck. You have lost your horse."

Soon after, the village wise man arrived, saying simply, "We shall see if this is good or bad."

Two days later, the horse returned to the farmer, bringing with it six wild horses. These new horses made the farmer very rich. His neighbors assured him, "This is very good luck. You started out with one horse, and now you have seven."

The wise man said simply, "We shall see if this is good or bad."

Days later, as the farmer's young son helped to break the wild horses, he was thrown to the ground and broke his leg.

"This is terrible luck," his neighbors declared. "Your son will be crippled. Such terrible misfortune!"

The wise man said again, "We shall see if this is good or bad."

The following week, the emperor's guard arrived to conscript all the young men of the village into the army. Because of his broken leg, the soldiers rejected the farmer's son, though they took every other young man. Perhaps the great misfortune was the young man's blessing.

While the story could go on and on, the point of the proverb is clear. At every turning point, the villagers want to judge events, declaring them either good or bad. Yet, what appears at first to be good turns out to be bad, and what appears at first to be bad turns out to be good. In truth, we don't *ever* have enough information to declare a verdict regarding an experience or situation—even in the face of what appears to be the most unfavorable situations. We must remember this in the face of our daily struggles.

One of my friends lost her husband after twenty years of marriage. He had a heart valve replacement followed by fibrillation, which ended in cardiac arrest. They were both young, very much in love, and looked forward to their empty-nest years together. His death sent her into two years of severe grief. Most of us would declare her husband's death a very bad event.

Seven years later, my friend sat through another funeral, this time watching a young grieving husband face life without the wife he'd loved. My friend told me, "I wanted so much to tell that husband that his life wasn't over. Though I wouldn't wish that pain on anyone, I knew it would get better for him. I'm so grateful for where I am today. Tim's death catapulted me into personal growth that changed the course of my life. If Tim had survived, I never would have become the woman I am."

Bad or good? Who knows, really? Mindfulness does not make a declaration in the middle of chaos any more than a doctor pronounces the sex of a baby before the infant's entire body has been delivered. Hold judgment. Doing so will allow you to experience mindfulness in a way that moves you toward resonance.

In the process of studying and practicing mindfulness, I've discovered something quite surprising. I realize that I have missed being fully present in much of my own life. While examining patients, charting notes, even during conversations with coworkers, my mind was always somewhere else—planning my rounds, considering a referral, or worrying about another patient.

I had been living my life without experiencing it—because I was never fully aware and present in the midst of it. Mindfulness changed that.

By observing myself and my world and silencing the chatter in my head, I grew more aware. I recognized the beauty in a child's smile, the gentleness of a mother's touch, the laughter of coworkers, and the glory of sun shining into my treatment rooms. Until I learned to pause and step back, these bits of beauty had completely escaped me.

Recently, I was asked to give a talk about stress at a local hospital. However, during rounds in another facility, I was unavoidably delayed. Concerned about the time, I hurried off to give my presentation. Already late, I drove toward my destination tense and anxious. I fretted, certain that everyone would think badly of me. Then, in a slap-yourself-on-the-forehead moment, the obvious occurred to me. I was going to give a talk on reducing stress while in the process of being stressed out. It was one of those laughable aha moments.

There in the car, I took a deep breath and deliberately stepped back from the rush of my anxious thoughts. I allowed myself to become fully aware of my body as I slowed my breathing and relaxed my muscles. I practiced gratitude and became aware of my surroundings. I chose to live in the moment, determined to fully experience that drive from Tacoma to Puyallup.

At that very instant, the fall leaves seemed to take on an almost eerie glow, and in the afternoon light, Mt. Rainier's majestic peak turned pink in the distance. In my anxiety and hurry, I'd almost missed the beauty of the extraordinary place I call home. I'd nearly driven through a postcard without recognizing and appreciating the beauty around me.

I am completely convinced that this practice not only changed my experience (enjoying the drive while being fully present) but also changed my presentation. By changing my focus and choosing to relax into a different physiological state, I was able to think with greater clarity, improving the quality of my presentation. I was able to more fully relate to the audience questions. I might add that on this occasion, when I arrived, I discovered that the schedule had been changed. I was not late after all!

Not only does mindfulness enable me to be fully present in my day, but it gives me greater access to my own creativity. During mindful moments, I often discover illusive and inventive solutions for the difficulties I face as a physician.

This remarkable access to creativity might be explained by research linking mindfulness with the neocortex, which is responsible for all higher reasoning, cognitive function, and language. Under stress, the body activates the reptilian brain (responsible for human survival—managing heart rate, breathing, body temperature, and balance) and the limbic system (responsible for our emotional life—the formation of memories, emotional triggers, and stress responses). The reptilian brain and the limbic system then dominate and override the neocortex (the center of higher cognition). By this process, the biochemistry of stress seriously impairs our higher thinking, reasoning, and creative problem-solving abilities. This purely physiological response can lead to catastrophic results.

With the neocortex off-line, people respond to stressors in unpredictable, even dangerous ways. In the heat of a burning building, with walls collapsing all around them, even familiar tools, such as emergency breathing apparatuses or radio control buttons can be confusing. When bullets fly through the air around him, a police officer may lose track of his reasoning or negotiation skills.

Experts have learned that in the midst of a true emergency, people find it difficult to think. The stress-driven physiological response, overriding the neocortex with its reasoning and creativity, explains the need for repeated emergency training drills. Police, EMTs, fire personnel, and emergency management groups regularly practice for terrorist threats, mass casualties, and active shooter events. Medical personnel drill relentlessly for cardiac code procedures and mass casualty events. Wildland fire personnel repeatedly rehearse donning fire shelters. With the repetition of these emergency drills, supervisors hope that emergency behaviors become so habitual that even in the worst of disasters, the accompanying stress won't override the routine of training.

You might wonder how, in the midst of a busy clinic day, with telephones ringing and a waiting room full of sick patients, anyone finds time for mindfulness. Many professionals don't even take time to eat lunch! Wouldn't mindfulness simply put you further behind schedule?

Not necessarily. As I have practiced mindfulness, I have become both more efficient and more effective. Mindfulness helps me to listen more fully. With a more accurate understanding of the problem, I can reason thoughtfully, identify and consider more than one solution, and make fully informed decisions. Instead of doing four things badly—believing that I am multitasking—I do one thing very well. That one thing goes more quickly, more successfully than when I have too many things crowding my awareness. The things I accomplish rarely come back to haunt me because they were done incompletely or inaccurately. With mindfulness, I find that I rarely have to redo my own work.

Should you choose to practice mindfulness, I suggest you begin first in nonstressful situations. Begin at home, resting in a comfortable chair. As you become aware of your breathing, listen to the air flowing in and out of your lungs. Pay attention to your surroundings. Notice details. As your mind wanders away to schedules and conflicts, gently bring it back to the present, calling attention again to your breath, your body, your posture, and your surroundings. With practice, you will keep your mind more focused and your body more relaxed. Gradually try to practice mindfulness in other places—as you sit in your car, as you walk outside, or as you visit with a loved one.

Eventually, as this becomes habitual, you'll find that you can be mindful even as chaos seems to roil around you. I have developed my own method from a poem by Vietnamese Buddhist priest Thich Nhất Hanh. His words have become a kind of mantra for me, providing a method for me to pause in the midst of difficulty and step back, moving into mindfulness. This technique doesn't demand a lot of time. With one breath, I find I can back away from the chaos.

> Breathing in, I calm body and mind.
> Breathing out, I smile.
> Dwelling in the present moment, I know this is the only moment.

Can three lines of a rather mundane poem change anything in any significant way? University of Massachusetts researcher Dr. Judson Brewer, a psychiatrist and neuroscientist, is trying to answer this very question. His results demonstrate a strong physiologic response to the deliberate thought control of mindfulness. By recording brain waves using a portable 128-electrode EEG, Brewer has discovered that the brains of subjects focused on job or schedule pressure show frenzied activity. When the same subjects drop into mindful meditation, this wild brain activity immediately quiets. By stepping back to quiet the mind and experience the moment, subjects reveal measurable changes to the activity in the brain.

By practicing mindfulness in the midst of my chaotic day, I find that I create space, a kind of virtual distance between a difficult experience and me. Stepping away from the agitation of the moment, I enter a place of poise, peace, and resonance. In this space, I make room for my inner wisdom to rise to the surface. Creative solutions to the problem become far more apparent. Even when I cannot change what is happening—as in the case of death or a catastrophic turn of illness—I find that I can present in such a way that I am able to bring my best self to the situation.

For me, one key result of mindfulness is the ability to release my expectations. As we have said, unmet expectations can be a key source of stress in the caring professions. In the past, working with patients, I frequently had an agenda. Whether my agenda included smoking cessation, freedom from alcohol, managing blood sugar, or beginning an exercise program, providing good health care always involved having specific objectives for each of my patients. When my goals weren't met, despite my best efforts, I frequently experienced frustration, anxiety, and occasionally even anger. But now, by using this gift of mindfulness, I am helped to release judgment. A situation is not good or bad, it simply is. I am able to remain engaged in a positive way. I am open to creative alternatives and able to continue having empathy and compassion for my patients.

MINDFULNESS AND COMPASSION FATIGUE

Repeated frustration, anxiety and even anger can contribute to what professionals call compassion fatigue. With a patient or client, we determine our best course of action and go above and beyond to provide the needed care—perhaps requesting unique insurance authorization, admission to a treatment facility, or a referral to a specialized provider. A teacher might put in extra effort, write the letters, make the additional phone calls, and go home late in order to provide extra services for a student. All too often, in spite of our best efforts, the patient or client or parent fails to follow through. The parent won't attend parenting classes. The student drops out of tutoring. How many physicians have admitted patients to drug or alcohol treatment only to find that they have checked themselves out of treatment the following day?

In the caring professions, it can be easy to take these outcomes personally, perhaps seeing them as personal failure—or worse, rejection. We end up resenting our patients or clients, convinced they don't appreciate our hard work. We may even wish we could get some of our time and effort back.

After experiencing these disappointments, we might become hesitant to work as hard for our next patient or client. Some part of us becomes jaded, less willing to go out of our way. We may begin to believe that eventually, all patients and clients will disappoint us. Believing this, we hold back, unwilling to interact personally with those in our care. As this hard edge grows inside us, we become less human and less compassionate. In the end, we are less effective.

By practicing mindfulness, I have learned to care without emotionalattachment. By this, I mean that I let go of my personal agenda. I can do whatever is necessary and then step back, allowing the patient to be exactly who he is at that moment along his own path. Unwilling to judge myself by the results of my care, I can give freely without the overwhelming need to control the results. As I practice mindfulness, I frequently imagine my hands open, palms up. By this gesture, I symbolize my emotional commitment to releasing my expectations.

Mindfulness frees me from judgmental words like *failure* or *ineffective* or *wasteful*. Mindfulness protects me from the stress and depression of compassion fatigue while allowing me the freedom to continue to work with and for those who might choose a better, stronger path but do not.

Practicing mindfulness has allowed me to release my reactive stressed out self. By identifying with my observer self, I approach life from a deeper space which enhances by spirituality. I can, by pausing and stepping back from my difficulty, let go and center myself. In this hyperaware state, I observe my surroundings, feel, and become aware of my own responses and the responses of the people around me. In this way, I allow the spiritual part of me to connect with the Divine and, through that connection, find courage and peace and gratitude. These emotional and spiritual gifts are amazing results of practicing mindfulness.

Chapter Eight
THE TOOL

> "Work is about a search for daily meaning as well as daily bread, for recognition as well as cash, for astonishment rather than torpor; in short, for a sort of life rather than a Monday through Friday sort of dying."
> Studs Terkel, *Stress and Quality of Working Life*, 2006

Now that you are familiar with the spiritual techniques that help us avoid complaining, resentment, and anxiety, I hope that you have begun to practice them. By now, I hope your gratitude has matured. Perhaps you're moving beyond being thankful for the ways your situation might be worse. Perhaps you now recognize the deeper, more valuable lessons that our difficulties teach us. As you practice forgiveness, you find you are more willing to let go of minor offenses. By forgiving the little things, you no longer accumulate irritations. The rush hour freeway is less stressful. Practicing mindfulness, you have begun to dwell below the tumult of frustrations caused by other people's inefficiencies or thoughtlessness.

However, even those who work at developing and growing their spirituality find that life continues to throw them occasional curveballs. No matter. The techniques I am about to share will allow you to experience even extremely difficult stressors without backing away or burning out. With practice, the skills you have begun to cultivate can be combined to create a new path for dealing with stress. In the analogy of baseball, this technique

The Tool

slows down the pitch, giving you time to think, to aim, and to swing accurately. I call this combination of techniques "the tool". Brilliantly creative, I know.

My clinical team is familiar with this simple phrase because we use it all the time. When things go badly, when the waiting room is full of unexpected patients or one of the staff goes home sick, leaving us overworked and understaffed, I tell them, "Time to work the tool."

I use it when one of my hospitalized patients takes an unexpected turn for the worse or when I'm facing the anxious parent of a very sick child. I use it when the board I serve makes a decision that strikes me as unproductive or even unwise. I've learned that by working the tool, I effectively manage my stress while accessing the best of who I am. In the process, I am not distracted by any one person's negative behaviors. With the tool, I remain calm and perform to the best of my ability.

You can better understand this concept if you imagine yourself as having two parts—an ego self and an essence self. Like the story of the two wolves, the two selves compete for dominance. The ego self is your reactive, protective self, tied to things related to your physical or outward well-being. The ego self is concerned with things like position, power, appearance, opinion, and possessions. It may also be driven by actual physical needs, such as hunger, exhaustion, or loneliness. More than anything, the ego self is driven to protect against loss—whether physical, financial, emotional, or reputational. The ego self is as likely to respond to rejection or disapproval as to hunger or danger.

Be careful not to label the ego self as entirely bad. It plays an important role in survival and must be loved and appreciated for its ability to give us strong signals about the safety of our environments. But the ego self is best kept under tight control. When the ego self dominates daily life, we find ourselves in a fight-or-flight existence.

Your essence self is your deepest self. This part of you is concerned for others, managing your emotions and interpreting your environment through spiritual eyes—eyes of service, connection, or calling. The essence self considers other opinions and perspectives. It is creative, open, and willing to give in order to help others. The essence self comes to the world from a place of love and wisdom.

Unfortunately, for most of us, the ego self demands most of our time and attention. I am often so busy protecting myself against harm that I forget the way back to my deepest and best self. That journey, from my ego self to my best self, is governed essentially by my spiritual awareness. Allowing my best self—my essence self, the self characterized by both wisdom and love—to dominate my daily life takes persistent work. My daily spiritual practices help me toward this goal. They move me from self-protection to generosity, from outward illusion to inner reality, and from reaction to love. But sometimes my daily spiritual practices don't help me in the flash of a difficult moment. I need something more. I need the tool.

As I use the tool (my private formula for getting back to my essence self), I allow my growing spirituality to move me from one space (self-protectiveness) to the other (love and generosity). At first, this shift is agonizingly slow and intentional. With practice, I have learned to make the shift more quickly. As the pattern becomes more ingrained and habitual, I find it can be nearly effortless.

Though the tool involves several steps, the whole process can be completed in just minutes. In the moment it takes to step back from your frustration, you can change your attitude and your response. As soon as I experience a crisis, whether in the clinic, with the staff, or with one of my patients, I move through several simple deliberate steps:

The Tool

1. Mindfulness: I step back, becoming aware of my thoughts and feelings without judging them.
2. Gratitude: I shift my mental focus from the details of the crisis to gratitude.
3. Forgiveness: I let go of my resentment toward those who caused this trouble.
4. Guidance: I open my mind and ask the Divine for creative solutions.

Let me show you, from a practical standpoint, how the tool might work. Imagine that as I arrive at work, I scan the schedule to discover that Mrs. Jones is booked for two o'clock in the afternoon. Immediately, I remember her last appointment and groan. Because I wouldn't provide additional narcotic pain medication for Mrs. Jones, our last meeting ended badly, with a discussion that escalated into an angry confrontation.

Without any way of moving from my ego self to my best self, I might feel deflated by the idea of seeing Mrs. Jones again. I might even resent the receptionist who had scheduled her appointment. On an ordinary day, my memories of our last visit would leave me anxious. I might begin to watch the clock, wishing time to slow down. I might begin to feel a professional malaise, a dissatisfaction and frustration about my work situation. In the old days, the days before the tool, I would have struggled with discouragement and anxiety throughout the morning, leaving my mind cluttered and unable to focus. No matter how the feelings progress, my ego self, the part of me that wants to avoid conflict and protect myself from false accusation, would have hijacked my attention; I couldn't have given my best to the patients I saw *before* Mrs. Jones's appointment.

But now there is another way.

As soon as I begin to experience these feelings of discomfort, dread, and even anger, I become aware of my own internal state. I observe my emotions without judgment or evaluation. The ego self, the protective self, is not my enemy. This part of my personality protects me from dangerous, unhealthy, or even abusive situations. My goal is to use the ego self to become *aware* of my feelings rather than to allow those feelings to control me. I may even name my feelings. However, I avoid identifying with them. Instead of "I am afraid," I might recognize "I'm feeling anxious."

My next step is to begin the shift back to my best self, my essence self. I begin this journey with gratitude. When I share this example with audiences, I ask them what I might be grateful for in the case of Mrs. Jones. The audience always suggests ways the situation might be worse, much worse.

- I don't have a whole schedule filled with people like Mrs. Jones.
- She only has one fifteen-minute appointment.
- I'm not married to Mrs. Jones.
- All health care involves people like Mrs. Jones. At least I have a job.

Though some of these are humorous, all of us can begin to be grateful by recognizing the ways something isn't as bad as it could be. These thoughts begin the flow of gratitude. With practice, you can begin to express gratitude in more evolved ways—recognizing the ways that all difficulty presents an opportunity for growth and change.

In the case of Mrs. Jones, I am thankful for the ways this particular patient has forced me to grow as a person and as a professional. I am thankful for the things she may teach me about her illness and its treatment. I am thankful for the way her experience with pain may help me take better care of others struggling with pain. I am thankful for the way she challenges me to be fully present and available to meet her real needs. I am thankful for another chance to work more successfully with her. Perhaps at this appointment I will be more empathetic or

THE TOOL

better able to explain why narcotic painkillers will not solve her problems. I am thankful that I have another chance to search for better options; perhaps this time we will find a more effective solution together.

As I dwell for a moment in gratitude, another thought strikes me: there but for the grace of God go I. As I see myself in this difficult patient—in her situation, in her entrapment—I let go of the resentment I feel toward her. This is the step of forgiveness. As I choose to forgive her past behavior, I discover that I must also forgive myself for my own feelings. I let go of the guilt I feel for judging her addiction. I let go of the guilt I feel for my resentment and frustration with my patient.

I open myself to the grace that is shown to me for my own shortcomings. As I accept that grace, I continue to let go of my protective emotions and behaviors.

In the last step of moving from ego to essence and toward my best self, I again use mindfulness to step away from my own emotions—whether they are anger, irritation, or frustration—and ask for divine presence and guidance. As I do this, I admit my own inability to solve this problem and open myself to deeper inspiration. Because my feelings and memories run deep, I may have to repeat this process several times over the course of my morning schedule.

By the time I enter Mrs. Jones's exam room, I feel calm and relaxed, centered in my best self. Though she begins our interaction by lashing out at me, I do not take her anger personally. Instead, I begin with honesty. "I'm sorry about how this process has gone for you. We haven't been able to help you as much as I'd have liked. If you agree, I'd like us to start over. This time, I hope we'll do much better at solving the problem."

My quiet, calm response deescalates our encounter, and during our time together, we make good progress. This meeting proceeds far more profitably than our last. Together, we consider other out-of-the-box treatments that might ease her physical pain.

Even now, after so many years of practice, I admit that I am not able to use the tool successfully all of the time. Occasionally, I still get caught off guard. Not all of my difficult experiences give me time to prepare as I did with Mrs. Jones. However, whenever I anticipate a difficult encounter, I can use the tool to my advantage. With practice, I am better able to step out of the ego self and into my calm, peaceful best self.

If you practice the tool, soon you will succeed at making the transition. You, like me, will experience several remarkable gifts. One of them is an ability to interact with those around you without taking things personally. Conflicts are always difficult enough without the additional stress of feeling blamed or inadequate. When we don't take things personally, we don't waste time defending ourselves. Instead, we move quickly to problem-solving, caring for others, or, if necessary, making past wrongs right.

Another gift of the transition is that in this calm, peaceful, loving place, we are able to avoid the stirred-up emotional state that keeps us from our own intuitive wisdom. We can hear this inner voice only when we quiet the chatter of an unsettled, emotion-filled mind. Resentment, anxiety, and upheaval rarely provide the kind of peace that allows our past experiences, associations, and wisdom to rise to the surface. When the mind and emotions are quiet and the body is not experiencing the fight-or-flight response, we have the presence of mind to ask and to listen for divine guidance. This can be a remarkable source of creative and even counterintuitive solutions.

What happens when difficult interactions catch us off guard? What about the curt response of a coworker or my own rude overreaction to conflict? These too can benefit from the tool.

The steps of the tool can be used whenever we become aware of our needs. Suppose that an unpleasant interaction catches me unexpectedly at the hospital. A nurse accuses me of leaving poor instructions. A family is angry about a bad patient outcome.

The Tool

Perhaps I react poorly, leaving the hospital angry, maybe even justified in my response. The nurse was rude to me. She didn't understand what I was trying to do. I am embarrassed that she spoke to me that way in front of other people.

At some point, I recognize that the event has left me with symptoms of fight-or-flight. My pulse is racing. I feel tension in my neck and shoulders. I may even feel the onset of a headache.

Even after the event has passed, I can still move through the steps of the tool. I allow myself to become fully aware of my emotions and of my body's response to the situation. I become mindful of these emotions without letting them own me. I acknowledge my feelings. I take a deep breath and let my emotions go, concentrating on my breathing as I step back emotionally. I focus on gratitude, moving toward more subtle and important reasons to be grateful for the difficult interaction or for the demanding persons involved. As I give thanks, I let go of my resentment, forgiving the rude remarks, even when they are my own. I try to understand what might have caused those emotions and behaviors. I deliberately forgive the one who has hurt me, freeing him or her from my own anger and bitterness. Then, as I pause and rest in my new emotional calm, I ask for divine guidance.

Often at this point I think of a solution to our conflict. Or, perhaps I perceive that I must take responsibility for my own behavior. I may have to go back to the person with whom I've behaved badly and ask forgiveness. I may need to make our relationship right in some important way. Whatever solution comes to mind, I have discovered that even hours or days after a difficult event I can move from the defensive, reactive ego self to a place where my best and most loving self emerges.

When the ego self dominates our actions, we humans often leave behind a trail of destruction—a virtual wake of damaged people. However, when we choose to reside in a good place, in the essence self, we not only make our own worlds a better place, we make the world better for all the people we contact—even strangers.

A friend of mine tells of pulling into a gas station with her fuel gauge on empty. "I'd been terrified that I'd run out of gas with four kids in the car," she explained. "So I didn't pull to the forward pump. I just dumped the car at the first pump and jumped out."

As she filled her tank, another car pulled in. The driver got out and let loose a tirade of anger. He was inconvenienced and offended that my friend hadn't pulled to the forward pump. Embarrassed, she didn't respond. As she went inside the station to pay, my friend used the tool to calm herself. With divine guidance, she went outside and apologized to the stranger.

"It was selfish to stop where I did. I was just so afraid I'd run out of gas," she explained. To her surprise, the stranger started to cry.

"I shouldn't have yelled at you," he said. "I'm just so upset lately. My wife left me; she wants a divorce."

The tool not only averted my friend's stress but also made a way for this overwhelmed stranger to return to his best self.

The tool can be valuable in other difficult interactions—even nonhuman ones. I've never been a fan of tests. Over the years, I've struggled with anxiety over my specialty board exams. Though I've certainly prayed about these regularly scheduled tests, before my last exam I'd never before applied the tool to my test experience. On that most recent exam, I decided that I would try the tool.

As I prepared, I recognized my negative emotions, holding them at arm's length without judging or criticizing myself. I practiced gratitude—expressing thanks for the opportunity to refresh my knowledge base, to test my new tool, and to keep my mind professionally sharp. On the day of the exam, I chose to be fully present in the moment. I focused on being aware of the classroom and of the attendant overseeing the test. As I smiled at her, I felt my body relax. I didn't give space to thoughts about whether I would pass. Instead, as I took the test, I practiced breathing, awareness, and prayer. I treated each question as though it were its own special game, separate from the other questions. Throughout my time in the examination, I found I worked every aspect of the tool. Remarkably, on this most recent test, I did better than I have ever done before.

You may not want to begin using the tool on your next stressful experience. Instead, practice the steps in the quiet of your own home. Begin by thinking about a problem you've recently experienced. Hold the problem in your mind, aware of your body's response and your emotions. Begin to express thanks for the difficulty. Move from "it could be worse," to higher expressions of gratitude. Forgive the offending person. Forgive yourself. Then, in this quiet, peaceful state, ask for divine guidance. Perhaps you will hear some unexpected bit of wisdom or direction. Follow that guidance and see what happens.

You can use the tool in the midst of a stressful experience. At first, it might not work perfectly. But with repetition, you'll find that you are less likely to dwell in and react from your ego self. Instead, your best self will rise to meet the difficulty. In the process, you will experience a much more peaceful and relaxed physiological state.

The tool helps us to move beyond fight-or-flight into peace. Because stress and frustration are primary contributors to burnout, the tool can help you ease those feelings and prevent the spread of emotional upheaval. Though using the tool successfully takes time and practice, eventually you will master these steps. Even as you learn, you will experience a more peaceful inner world.

Chapter Nine
UNDERSTANDING THE TOOL ELEMENTS

> "I think the first step is to understand that forgiveness does not exonerate the perpetrator. Forgiveness liberates the victim. It's a gift you give yourself."
> TD Jakes, *Let It Go: Forgive So You Can Be Forgiven*

MORE ON FORGIVENESS

Because forgiveness is a vital part of the tool, I want to expand and clarify the term. True forgiveness does not condone another person's bad behavior. It doesn't excuse that behavior by explaining it away—even when we can trace the behavior to some previous experience or difficulty.

As we forgive, we deliberately choose to let go of our bitterness and anger generated by our painful experiences. In the process, we release our desire for retribution or retaliation. It has been said that forgiveness frees us from the endless longing for a different outcome. I like that definition. By letting go, the past no longer controls our present. Doing this emasculates our hurts, preventing past pain from stealing our present joy. Forgiveness is a pathway by which we move forward, letting go of old injuries and the emotions that go with them. This process provides a way to move beyond whatever has happened to us.

You may have heard the expression "forgive and forget." This phrase implies that the effects of forgiveness will be instant and complete. I have found that even those who have forgiven may continue to experience feelings of regret or sadness. We should expect this; after all, we are human. Forgiveness means simply that we have chosen not to let our feelings drive our actions or responses. And many offenses one should not forget. It is also important to have boundaries.

Forgiveness is not easy. The more severe the offense, the more difficult the forgiveness process will be. For severe injuries, forgiveness does not come in a single moment but via a series of decisions, choosing over and over again to let go of the offense. In some cases, an injured person might benefit from the assistance of a counselor or close friend. In my observation, a past wound sometimes makes us more sensitive to other offenses only vaguely related to the original offense. It takes courage to work through these tough issues and find the real source of discomfort. Only the truly brave have the perseverance to hang on until they experience freedom.

Unfortunately, some never try.

One day in my clinic I cared for a patient presenting with several difficult medical conditions. She was bitter and angry, and I suspected that many of her medical issues were likely related to her deep-seated emotional struggles. At one point in our conversation, I gently asked about her faith. Her answer was both swift and virulent.

"I hate God," she said. Then she shared her story:

Years before our meeting, a terrible accident had claimed the lives of several of her cousins. She blamed God for the accident and couldn't get over the injustice of so many young lives unnecessarily lost. Her bitterness and anger toward God pervaded her emotional life. She was as angry on the day we spoke as she might have been if the event had occurred the day before.

After we spoke, I wondered if she would ever recognize that the dead children were not the only lives lost in the accident. Anger and bitterness had not only destroyed this woman's health but had stolen most of her adult life as well.

A few days later, I went into another treatment room where I found a young man severely affected by injuries sustained in a childhood accident. Those injuries had left him with a severe and painful disability. His chronic use of pain medication eventually led to drug addiction. Through hard recovery work, the young man had struggled with and overcome his drug habit. Though I'd cared for him for some time, I hadn't really recognized the elements of his story. That day in the exam room, I realized that that this young man had actually been involved in the accident my previous patient described. His deformity, pain, addiction, and recovery were direct results of that horrific event.

But the young man did not view himself as a victim. Instead, he considered himself a survivor. Though his injuries left him with lifelong difficulties, he was grateful to be alive. He believed that he had a divine call to help other young people struggling with addiction. He did not deny his past. Admittedly, the accident had shaped his life. However, his feelings about what had happened did not control his present. The young man chose forgiveness over blame.

The glaring difference between these two people struck me as remarkable. Though the accident did not directly affect this woman, she chose to blame God for it, living a bitter, angry, unforgiving life. The young man was directly and deeply wounded by the accident, yet he chose forgiveness. As a result, he experienced peace. Viewed through the lens of forgiveness, the accident had given him a life calling, a divine purpose that added meaning to his otherwise unfocused life.

In his book titled *Buddha's Brain: The Practical Neuroscience of Happiness, Love, and Wisdom,* author Rick Hanson makes a remarkable statement about the power of negativity. Negativity, he declares, is like Velcro, attracting and sticking to any oncoming negative thought or experience. On the other hand, positive thinking provides an almost Teflon-like resistance to the influences of difficult situations, circumstances, and people.

Positive thinking, in Hanson's point of view, inoculates us to the venom of stress and conflict.

This neurological observation may be more than an encouragement to Pollyanna thinking. It may explain why an angry or awkward encounter with a coworker at the start of the day progresses into a day filled with additional frustration, disappointment, and difficulty. By holding on to the initial insult, the negative attitude continues to attract and label other experiences and interactions as negative or unpleasant. By the end of the day, these experiences accumulate like lint on Velcro until you feel nothing but frustration and disappointment. If one bad interaction can change how we perceive an entire day, why wouldn't a long series of bad days change our entire perception of our work?

This kind of escalation makes overcoming negative perceptions even more critical in preventing burnout. The three habits of gratitude, forgiveness, and mindfulness do far more for us than simply replacing complaining, resentment, and anxiety. Gratitude moves us into a more peaceful emotional state. Forgiveness changes our focus, allowing us to let go of the negative emotions we experience as a result of the things that happen to us. As we make these choices, we view the bigger picture, opening ourselves to new direction and purpose. By becoming aware of our internal worlds, mindfulness allows us to *choose* our responses rather than *be controlled by* our circumstances. Together, these habits determine the direction and color of our worlds.

INTUITIVE GUIDANCE: CAN YOU TRUST IT?

Many great artists, among them Johann Sebastian Bach, Joseph Haydn, Rembrandt, and Michelangelo, linked their remarkable creativity with divine service and inspiration. Bach wrote the initials S. D. G. (Full Latin Word: Soli Deo Gloria, meaning To the Glory of God) at the beginning of all his church and many of his secular works. George Frideric Handel wrote this inscription as well.

In today's business vernacular, creativity has become the golden goose. Team leaders are looking for applicants who demonstrate outstanding creativity. Creativity drives innovative product research, design, and marketing. In response, much expensive research has been conducted to discover how big business can foster creativity via environment, internal culture, attitudes, and educational resources. Creativity tops the list of the twenty most watched TED Talks of all time. Schools, cities, and even scientific research teams are seeking ways to enhance human creativity and problem-solving.

These same researchers might be quick to discard the concept of creative guidance stemming from our spiritual connection with the Divine. Certainly this source of creativity defies standard research methods. Yet, we shouldn't overlook our spirituality as a possible source for creative solutions to nagging problems. Once, as I was presenting this material to a group of health-care professionals, I took audience questions. A brave young woman raised her hand. "I just want to ask how you *know* if this stuff is really true."

Her point is valid. How can anyone be truly confident of spiritual issues, especially the question of divine guidance or intuitive guidance? Without being able to document these sources, how can we know that they work?

When it comes right down to it, issues of spiritual or intuitive guidance all depend on some level of trust. Many spiritual truths are difficult to prove scientifically, such as the power of love. For each of us, trust is a very personal issue. Trust is something we must come to individually.

If you choose trust, no one can argue your trust away. If you cannot or will not trust, no outside persuasion will change your mind. Those who do not trust will likely never be convinced. I present this opportunity for spiritual or divine guidance as a possibility you might want to consider. Perhaps you will discover more than meets the eye.

I answered this woman's question as honestly as I could. "You are completely correct. No one can ever prove that there is a spiritual dimension to our human existence." I let that statement hang. "But what I know with certainty is that I've *experienced* the spiritual side of my own humanity. And when it comes to intuitive guidance, I have dozens of examples of situations when I've received answers completely outside of my own wisdom or training. It happens regularly—far too regularly—for me to doubt my ability to connect with this wisdom that is beyond myself and to receive something, some creative answer, that is far beyond my own problem-solving ability."

I remember an appointment I had with a patient who was truly suffering. Unable to find real relief, he'd amassed a virtual army of specialists who had not provided any additional insight. No matter what approach these professionals suggested, my patient had not recovered his health. When I saw him on my schedule, I'll be honest. I was a little bewildered. After all, if so many specialists couldn't help him, what did I have to offer?

Before I entered his exam room, I worked the tool. Aware of my churning emotions, I chose to be fully present in the hallway— aware of the moment, aware of my own doubts, and aware of the potential in the encounter. I gave thanks for the opportunity to see this patient and considered the possibility that I might be used to bring something new to my patient's experience. Then, in the quiet of the hallway, I silently asked for guidance.

As I talked with the patient, I continued to be fully present, listening intently as he explained his most recent difficulty. I asked questions, keenly aware of ideas as they popped into my thoughts. Suddenly, a specific medication came to my mind. As we continued to talk, I wondered whether this medicine might help my patient. Part of me wanted to dismiss the idea. Certainly other specialists had already considered this pharmaceutical solution. Maybe it wasn't such a good idea after all.

When the appointment was over, I called the patient's cardiologist and suggested this medication. "I don't think it will help," he responded. "But you can try it if you want to. It won't hurt anything."

Aware that this solution might have come from wisdom beyond my own, I prescribed the medication. To my amazement, the patient began to recover. This unexpected suggestion, one that other specialists had already dismissed, came from our appointment together—the one when I took the time to ask for guidance.

I have experienced what I call intuitive guidance in ways far too numerous to list. But rather than illustrate the principle with my own experiences, I've chosen to include others here:

Maggie, who considers herself an intensely spiritual person, serves as an ICU nurse at a large downtown Seattle hospital. "I have no question that I experience guidance in my work. Sometimes, I stop to ask for it. Other times, it seems to interrupt me with inspiration for approaches I'm not smart enough to think of on my own."

In one situation, Maggie, who works nights, had spent much of her shift struggling to increase her patient's systolic blood pressure, which was hovering in the seventies. "I needed to get more medicine on board if I hoped to save this patient," she explains.

She consulted with the hospital's intensive care specialist, obtaining orders for the placement of a central line. Shortly afterward, a surgical resident placed the line under ultrasound guidance. A postprocedure chest X-ray confirmed the line's placement into the superior vena cava, and the resident told Maggie that she could use the line to deliver her medications. Both the intensivist and a radiologist examining the X-ray came to the same conclusion. Normally, that would be all the medical authority Maggie needed to begin using the line for delivering the additional medicine.

But for some reason, on this occasion, Maggie decided to check the pressure in the line itself, using the CVP waveform as proof of perfect placement. It is important to note that in her five years as a critical care nurse specialist, Maggie had never before felt the need to do this. But she couldn't shake the feeling that she should check. When she did, the test results did not show the venous pressure she expected. Instead, the waveform indicated that the line had been placed into an artery.

Surprised, Maggie asked her nursing supervisor to recheck her work. The supervisor confirmed Maggie's findings. Then Maggie requested the intensivist repeat the test. Everyone agreed that during the placement, the central line had actually perforated the target vessel, passing completely through the vein and into the artery lying just behind it.

Had Maggie not checked the line's placement, she would have delivered vasoconstrictive medication directly into the patient's brain, with catastrophic results. This inner hesitation followed by the clear impulse to proceed in a direction other than her normal routine probably saved her patient's life.

"I'm not that smart," Maggie told me, smiling. "I wouldn't have thought of it on my own. I really think I had divine intervention, divine wisdom, a prompting to do something outside of my own routine. I'm grateful that I listened to that inner voice."

Doug, a Seattle police officer, reports a slightly different kind of experience with this type of guidance. One night, anticipating his night shift break, Doug headed toward his usual convenience store where he planned to have coffee with the clerk. As he pulled his police car into the lot, a radio request interrupted his plans. A nearby pastor had called police, worried about a homeless person who had just set up camp on the church steps.

Frustrated that he would miss his coffee break, Doug put the car in reverse and headed out to answer the call. "I'm a little embarrassed about how mad I was. I didn't want to go bust a homeless guy. I wanted my coffee. I wanted to sit down and chill out. Aware of my own anger, I felt myself winding up, thinking, *It isn't going to go well for this guy.*"

Climbing out of his patrol car, Doug was hit by a blast of night wind. "As the air blew over me, I was overtaken by this strange compassion. It wasn't mine. It came with this deep peace and an unusual calmness. Instantly, my anger was gone. I knew I'd experienced a holy moment."

Doug found the man camping out on the church steps, just as the dispatcher had described. Introducing himself, Doug began, "I'm sorry," he said. "I'm nervous about you being here. I have to ask you to leave. Is there somewhere I can take you?"

"I'd really appreciate it," the man responded. "There is a place I can go, but I can't get there by myself." The homeless man had been accepted into a treatment program scheduled to start on Monday.

Doug helped him into his patrol car and delivered him to the safe house. Later, by police radio, Doug heard that the man had left a box of his possessions on the church steps. "I still hadn't gotten that cup of coffee," Doug says, "but I headed back to that church and picked up his stuff. Then I drove it back to where I'd left him. That was divine compassion, not mine. It came from somewhere outside of myself."

While Doug's experience may have made no real difference to the homeless man, Doug's connection with the Divine changed his work experience. As a handler for his police dog, Doug says, "Normally, my job is very methodical. I just follow the dog until I find the bad guy. But this experience was something altogether different. I had a faith encounter, and I was the one who changed."

What began as an unwelcome interruption evolved into an experience of unusual compassion, allowing Doug to reach out to someone who desperately needed his kindness. In the process, Doug's police work went from being repetitive, ineffective, and boring to something meaningful and life-changing. Remarkably, the life most changed was Doug's own. Listening to our intuitive guidance can transform difficult and demanding work from drudgery to adventure. It can help us see that we are making a difference in a difficult world. Guidance can provide unusual answers and give us courage, strength, and compassion. Cultivating and responding to intuitive guidance has the potential to restore our passion for the work we do.

FOLLOWING INTUITIVE GUIDANCE TAKES COURAGE

Some people believe that courage is the remarkable strength that enables humans to face difficulty, pain, or danger *without* fear. The truth is more nuanced; without fear, there is no need for courage. Courage does the right thing, the difficult thing, the scary thing, even in the face of nerve-rattling fear.

Courage always involves risk. Sometimes risks can be calculated—like the risk of a building collapse or a line-of-fire risk. However, even with the best planning, risk is hard to pin down. A ricocheting bullet is hard to anticipate.

And so it is with intuitive guidance. Facing a difficult patient or an overwhelming circumstance, we work toward gratitude, forgiveness, and mindfulness. As we move into this place of resonance and inner peace, we become the best versions of ourselves. We are free of wild or destructive emotions, controlling ambition, anger, and bitterness.

In this moment of peace, we are open and undisturbed. From a place of love and wisdom, in this peaceful, quiet state, we seek direction and wait for wisdom to surface. Only then can we sense the answer. Perhaps the suggestion you hear is not conventional protocol. Perhaps there is risk involved—risk to the patient, to the group you work with, to you, or to your reputation. Perhaps you might even risk losing your job. What is your response? Do you follow the guidance you hear?

In her book *Eat, Pray, Love,* author Elizabeth Gilbert describes a night of sobbing on her bathroom floor, which she had done every single night for many, many weeks, desperate about the state of her life and marriage. Her husband wanted to start a family. Elizabeth wasn't even sure she wanted to stay married.

On the night in question, between hacking sobs, the author says she begged God for an answer. In a still small voice, Elizabeth heard, "Go back to bed, Liz." Gilbert believed that in an immensely practical way, God knew that when the tempest arrived, she would need her strength. The most practical thing to do, God insisted, was to go back to bed and get some rest.

Sometimes, inner wisdom gives us the most practical solutions.

At other times, we sense more complicated, even daunting solutions. What if the idea doesn't work? What will people think? What if I fail? What if we lose ground? It is only human to be cautious when we face fear. Fear of failure, fear of loss, fear of criticism—these are important risks. As caring professionals, we want more than anything to be helpful; at the same time, we desperately want others to demonstrate appreciation for our help. Following inner guidance carries an additional risk for those in the helping professions. What if that appreciation is transformed into disapproval or even rejection?

These are just the beginning of doubts. We believe that we are what others say about us, so we strive to have others approve. Following intuitive guidance, we risk staff disapproval, peer disapproval, and even client disappointment. Driven to succeed, we avoid the unpredictable paths that might lead to public failure. Following intuitive or divine guidance requires courage to overcome these very real and powerful fears.

I know these fears. I have experienced them. Though I cannot give you courage, I can tell you where I have found mine. When I wrestle with the decision to follow through on intuitive guidance,

Understanding the Tool Elements

I focus on the Divine's love for me and for my patients. Over the years, as I've responded to the guidance I've received, I've witnessed amazing, even wondrous results. I keep that in mind as I consider my options.

At other times, when my courage has failed me, I've experienced disappointment and regret. Looking back at those times, I can't help but ask myself, "What if... What if I'd done it? What if I'd done that crazy or surprising thing? What might have happened? What good thing did I miss?"

Sometimes, these moments of guidance seem almost insignificant. I remember some time ago I struggled to find solutions for one particular patient. During the evening, I felt the strongest sense that I should return to the hospital. No doctor wants to return to the hospital unnecessarily; I'm no different. But on this occasion, I felt compelled. In the quiet of the evening, I sat at the patient's bedside where he and I shared a long and surprising conversation. During our talk, we experienced a different kind of connection. From that conversation, an idea emerged—something I had not yet considered. That idea led to a solution that turned out to be key for my patient.

You'd think that after all these years, I would be adept at following my inner voice. Yet, sometimes I hesitate. Occasionally, I tell myself that my idea comes only from my own silly imagination ... or heartburn. Yet, this I know: when I ignore that voice, I have learned that I will always experience the same emotion—regret. I am left wondering what might have happened. Have I circumvented some surprising outcome simply by ignoring that voice?

When I work the tool and receive unanticipated guidance, I know I must follow through. Choosing to ignore that guidance denies the value of the extraordinary gift that is intuitive guidance. Taking action requires courage—though it is much easier now, after so many gratifying experiences.

Following that voice has led to great adventures, to surprising coincidences, and to unusual and heartwarming interactions with fellow staff members, residents, and patients. These results represent a remarkable synchronicity that characterizes much of my work. The right answers appear exactly when they are needed. The right people seem to arrive as if they've been directed by some unseen hand.

Intuitive guidance does not eliminate conflict and stress. Rather, it provides a path by which I can effectively deal with stressors. These kinds of experiences renew my sense of wonder and anticipation about my work.

Every day as I use the tool, I wonder,
What adventure lies ahead for me today?

Chapter Ten
ATTITUDE: IT'S WHAT WE MAKE OF IT

"We can complain because rose bushes have thorns,
or rejoice because thorn bushes have roses."
Abraham Lincoln

When I was a kid growing up in Japan, we used to spend our summer vacations on the coast. At the seaside we devoted long hours to a sport lying somewhere between boogie boarding and surfing. Our boards were made of inflatable canvas rectangles, about thirty by forty-eight inches. They weren't strong enough to support our standing weight. Instead, we knelt down, riding wave after wave after wave. I still remember the fun of those ancient toys and the hours we spent in the water.

Because of those memories, I especially value this quote from epic surfer, magazine writer, and editor Drew Kampion: "Life is a wave. Your attitude is your surfboard. Stay stoked and aim for the light."

According to Kampion, life is all about attitude. We can't choose the waves we face. Some are small and inconsequential. Others are towering giants, carrying great potential for danger. The really big waves can pick you up and toss you onto the rocks, or they can drag you under, pin you down, and kill you. With the right board and a little skill, those same waves can thrill like no other.

Like Kampion, I believe that our attitudes help us to ride the waves of our lives, no matter where you work. Firefighters, nurses, teachers, social workers—and anyone else who serves other human beings—struggle with the overwhelming demands we face. We serve fellow humans who've made poor choices. We often have to do our jobs without adequate funding, resources, and support. It's tempting to let negative self-talk bubble up:

- This is a waste of my time.
- This job is a pain.
- I'm sick and tired of this.
- Nothing I do really matters.

This kind of thinking leaves us feeling helpless and discouraged, trapped in a space where we are less than our best. When we can't change the waves we face, our only hope is to change our surfboards. But how do we change our attitudes? How can anyone stop in the midst of a crashing wave and swap out his surfboard?

Because each of us think and feel and react differently, the techniques you develop will be uniquely your own. To help you get started, I'll share my process with you here, suggesting some methods I've gleaned from other people as well. Feel free to take whatever suggestions seem effective. Expand them. Apply them to your specific situation. The one thing I can guarantee is this: the more often you swap out your board, making an important attitude shift, the more naturally and quickly the process will occur.

For me, the first step in making an attitude adjustment is to take a step back, moving from participant to observer. When I feel overwhelmed or stressed, I know that I must do something to step out of the pressure of the moment. I do this by pausing to attend to my own thoughts, judging their accuracy. This may surprise you.

Most of us automatically assume that all of our thoughts are real and that they are true. We identify completely with them (I am angry. I can't help it!), allowing them to take us deeper into unhealthy emotions, such as anxiety, resentment, frustration, and discouragement. We rarely—if ever—question them.

With time, I've learned that my thoughts are not always true or honest. Sometimes they don't even reflect reality. My thoughts are just thoughts. I derive my thoughts from my perceptions. By holding my perceptions at arm's length, I refuse to simply accept them as true or unalterable. At a distance, I am free to make a choice about which thoughts and feelings I allow to follow my initial perceptions.

When we find ourselves in difficult emotional states, having a spiritual perspective gives us the ability to pause and breathe. By stepping back, we observe our thoughts, deliberately shifting from participant to observer. From the observer perspective, we have a new ability to question the reality of those thoughts. Some people begin this shift by immediately questioning their own conclusions or thoughts about the crisis, asking key questions like, "Is that absolutely true?"

We humans are quick to make assumptions about the motives of others. We quickly interpret the meaning or significance of a disappointment. When a spouse is late, we might determine, "He's late because I'm not important to him." A bad performance review might lead us to conclude, "I'm going to lose my job." In the recesses of our thoughts, we manage to turn our anticipation of a bad result into fact, amplifying those facts into states of depression or anxiety. The brain believes these dark facts, leading us to a state of fight-or-flight. These dark emotions didn't happen spontaneously. They evolved from the faulty conclusions we tell ourselves about the events we experience. Asking myself the right question can effectively short-circuit my inaccurate and unprofitable thinking.

Your first task is to discover a way to stop yourself in the midst of your immediate reaction so that you can quickly become an observer of your own thoughts and emotions. I encourage you to find some simple phrase that you can repeat to yourself every time you face crisis. I've listed some suggestions here:

- In every crisis there is opportunity.
- Not everything is as it seems.
- Important things are not always visible.
- I will respond rather than react.
- Growth comes from discomfort.
- Struggle produces strength.

After I tell myself one of these truths, I take the next step, which is to quiet my reactive self and move toward my best self, my more loving and giving self. I make this shift by immediately asking myself another question: *What can I be thankful for? How can I find opportunity in this difficulty?* Even when I am feeling anxious or upset, I recognize that there is potential in any situation. With these questions, I begin to look for the silver lining in my cloud.

One of my Native American patients occasionally participates in the native Sun Dance, a feature of many Plains Indian tribes. For most tribes, this ceremony features music, dancing, and sacrifice for the healing of the tribe and its members. In some groups, the participant pierces the skin of his chest with two leather thongs—one on each side of the torso. The thongs are attached to a ceremonial pole, around which the celebrant dances as he prays. This dance continues for some time until, for some celebrants, the thongs literally pull through the skin of the chest wall, setting him free. These rituals are so sacred that details are rarely made public. However, my patient tells me that early in his experience, he understood the prayer for this ceremony to be translated, "Have mercy on me." More recently, he discovered that the truest meaning of the Lakota prayer used during the ceremony is this: "Make me a more compassionate being." From the pain and prayer, the participant seeks compassion.

I find this remarkable. For many of us, trauma leads us down the road of unforgiveness and bitterness. When I struggle with some painful event, compassion is rarely my first concern. Instead,

I fight against inconveniences, difficulties, and frustrations. But when I think back, I realize that my most strenuous difficulties have frequently led me to become more compassionate toward those who suffer. If we manage to make the shift, changing our perceptions of our struggles, we might recognize the remarkable opportunity our struggles provide us. Through struggle, we find the most valuable of rewards: compassion.

In nature, we see this same principle clearly illustrated in the life cycle of the butterfly. The larva creates his own chrysalis, a virtual tomb of inconvenience and difficulty, but when the time is right, the new creature must climb out by its own strength. This process helps the butterfly grow strong wings and healthy lungs. No doubt you have heard that assisting in this process proves fatal to the butterfly. The same is true for the hatching chicken or baby sea turtle. This law of nature—that struggle produces strength—provides another reason for us to cherish the struggles of everyday life.

Sometimes struggle creates a product of remarkable beauty. That beauty can be ours when we recognize a problem, reperceive that problem, and address it in new and creative ways. A pearl is nothing more than an irritation continuously attended to by a responsive oyster. As the oyster makes the best of an invasive particle of sand, it coats the sand with nacre (the same mineral that forms the mollusk's shell). This process of irritation and response eventually produces the lustrous, iridescent surface of a valuable gem. Without irritation, there would be no pearl. Not every oyster has this remarkable ability—just a precious few.

I admit that shifting my attitude doesn't come naturally. In days past, when my computer has frozen or crashed, my day crashed as well. How could I finish my work while unable to access the very tools I needed to complete those tasks? During these computer events, I struggled with levels of anger that surprised me. Ordinarily, I'm a pretty happy guy; however, any one of these crashes had the potential to completely ruin my day.

In one instance while charting important patient notes on my computer, the screen froze. At first, I was frustrated, even angry. Pushed for time, I couldn't afford to wait through this inconvenience. Then, remembering my own advice, I decided to swap my surfboard. I paused, breathed deeply, and centered myself. I began to give thanks for these unexpected moments of downtime. I headed to the restroom, which made my bladder very happy. When I returned, my computer remained frozen.

Unable to complete my task, I began to sort through a pile of paperwork on my desk. As I worked my way down the stack, I discovered a misplaced request that required my urgent attention and took action. Recognizing the silver lining, I paused to give thanks. Without the aid of my unwanted computer glitch, this buried request would never have been completed on time. As moments passed, I felt myself moving from the fight-or-flight zone into a place of peace and gratitude. By the time my system rebooted itself and I began seeing patients again, I felt relaxed and able to perform my best work.

On that day, I learned a big lesson. My response to these inconveniences *could* be changed. I decided to make a stronger effort. I began to start my day by blessing both my computer and our work together. Of course, I did not believe that this electronic vehicle would miraculously behave itself. Instead, I began to ask that I would see these interruptions in a new light, allowing them to change me in important ways. These days, I don't have to bless my computer anymore. My perspective has completely changed. I have a new surfboard.

Sometimes things don't happen in the way that you would choose. Some years ago we needed to add another staff physician. I felt it was best to hire another family practice physician. I reasoned that adding this specialty would allow us to provide broad coverage to all the patients we serve—from newborns to the elderly. As I wrote the job description for the new position, I received a directive from the tribal council, who served as our health board, to find and hire a pediatrician. I was frustrated and troubled.

The decision to hire a pediatrician made no sense to me. In our understaffed and overworked clinic, a family practice specialist would be the most obvious and efficient use of limited funding. In spite of my objections and appeal, the directive remained. I rewrote the job description and began the search for a competent candidate.

Eventually, we hired an excellent pediatrician. As I look back over that tumultuous period, I recognize this to be one of the most important and effective decisions the council has ever made. The pediatrician we hired is a wonderful and big-hearted physician. As a result of this individual's work, we have expanded our immunization program and our presence in the schools and developed programs for health promotion and disease prevention. Our immunization rates have dramatically improved.

This experience taught me much about trust. I have learned to recognize that there is a Great Wisdom beyond my own. Sometimes that wisdom comes via unexpected events and difficulties. Instead of fighting the situation, these and other experiences have taught me to let go and look for opportunity in the difficulty. Opportunity often leads to surprising and unexpected results.

The problem with trust is that it is far easier to talk about than to live out. Trust requires that we let go of our own expectations about how things ought to be. It requires being open to solutions we might never have experienced any other way.

There is an old story about a monkey who steals food from a poor jungle village. Unwilling to let the monkey continue eating their food, the villagers try to catch the thief. For some time, the little rascal evades them until a wise old man teaches the villagers this secret trick:

"Put food in the bottom of a narrow-mouthed clay pot," he instructs the villagers. "Then fasten the pot to a tree and go to bed." The next morning, to their utter surprise, the villagers discover a very angry monkey with his hand stuck inside the mouth of the clay pot. Except for his tightly fisted hand, the monkey might have run away. Because he would not let go of the food, the villagers could catch and dispose of the monkey.

Sometimes, like that monkey, we cannot let go of our own expectations, attitudes, and beliefs. Holding on to them, like a monkey to his food, those mental fists keep us trapped, unable to enjoy moments of joy and peace. Firmly held expectations and attitudes may even prevent us from discovering the secret wisdom or remarkable freedom exposed by either a small inconvenience or an overwhelming difficulty.

Letting go of offenses is a choice that we must make not just once, or even daily, but many times every single day. If we can learn the secret of stepping back, doubting the truth about our own conclusions, and then choosing to let go and trust, we can acquire a new attitude—a new surfboard.

One day, as I was considering the power of my thoughts, I recognized that with every stressor I faced, I had a choice. My decision about that choice would lead, like falling dominos, toward either further stress and unhappiness or, by contrast, toward my best self. At the time, I pictured these two contrasting pathways as leading me either downward toward discontent and frustration or upward toward peace and inspiration.

It isn't hard to picture. In the course of my work, I might struggle with a series of difficult events—perhaps an unmanageable workload or a demanding and unappreciative boss—and before I am even aware of it, I have begun the downward spiral toward further unhappiness and stress.

I am not talking here about one unpleasant afternoon. We all have those. Sometimes we react badly. Rather, this downward spiral describes what happens as we face a series of professional difficulties or setbacks and consistently choose to let the ego self have control over our responses. Via multiple encounters and successive decisions, we develop a repetitive way of thinking, a pattern leading to burnout.

In the other pattern, by choosing different responses, we experience challenge, growth, and freedom. The negative pattern I call the Descending *D*s, which leads us toward hopelessness.

THE DESCENDING *D*S

1. Define negatively. In this pattern, my difficulty is followed first by thoughts that use broad, overgeneralized language to express my unhappiness about the situation. These expressions might sound like this: "This isn't fair," "This job is too hard," or, "No one appreciates what I do."

By defining my experience negatively, my thoughts begin the downward spiral. Remarkably, the more absolute my negative conclusions, the faster my successive thoughts free-fall. Like an airplane accelerates toward the earth, it becomes more and more difficult to pull out of my emotional dive. At the same time, these negative thoughts drive my body toward fight-or-flight and ever deeper into physical stress, exhaustion, and burnout.

2. Discouragement. At this point, I may begin to recall other insults and mull them over in my mind. I remember the time my supervisor corrected me in front of coworkers. The time he added unpaid expectations to my workload. I let my mind dwell on the ways my work is not what I expected, emphasizing the gap between reality and expectations.

3. Disillusionment. As I move into disillusionment, I begin to believe that I am powerless to change my situation. My coworkers won't change. The job won't get better. I can't possibly make a difference in this environment. No one will ever appreciate the gifts I bring to the workplace. At this point, my ability to problem-solve has been severely compromised. I am no longer open to new ideas, to creativity, or to problem-solving.

4. Depression. By this stage, all joy in my work has vanished. I feel less energy. If I allow these deteriorating thoughts to continue, I may begin to dread going to work. I long for days off or an extended vacation. My hours at work begin to feel like a prison sentence. I begin to wonder if I will ever feel work satisfaction again.

5. Despair. The final stage of the Descending Ds involves the loss of hope. By now, the loss of energy and creativity has left me with absolutely no hope for solving my situation. My workplace is more than bad; it is hopelessly unchangeable. At this point, my only hope lies in getting out, either from this particular workplace or perhaps even from my profession.

By allowing these Ds—definition, discouragement, disillusionment, depression, and despair—to progress unchecked, I have given myself over to the stressors I experience at work. The process has amplified my distress. It is a sure recipe for burnout. But there is a better way.

THE ASCENDING AS

This pathway has the potential to transform our difficult moments into vehicles that move us beyond frustration. By making the most of our experiences and growing through them, we become the best version of ourselves. The process might look something like this:

1. Awareness. As I face a series of difficult encounters, instead of labeling the difficulties in a negative way, I choose to hold my emotions in awareness, observing them as if they belonged to someone else. Perhaps I feel disappointed or used. As I become aware of these feelings, I take a step back and acknowledge them. Rather than identifying with my feelings by saying, "I'm overwhelmed," I might say something like, "I'm feeling overwhelmed." I am careful not to judge myself and careful *not* to tell myself what I should or shouldn't feel.

2. Appreciation. Having acknowledged my emotions, I begin to cultivate thanks for something related to the difficulty. Even if I begin with the low-hanging fruit of gratitude (it could be worse), I take a moment to give thanks. I might start with, "At least most days aren't like this." The real trick, and the sign that I am becoming more competent in the area of gratitude, comes when I begin to look for opportunity in the midst of difficulty. To accomplish this, I may have to take a moment away, quieting myself and asking for divine help. "What positive outcome might develop out of this difficulty?"

3. Anticipation. At this point, using my thoughts about the potential benefits, I gather enthusiasm for the inherent potential I see. I begin to cultivate a vision for this positive outcome—something that might happen only *because* of this difficulty. My enthusiasm might sound like this: "Having patients stack up like this might give my supervisor the statistics he needs to demonstrate our need for more staff." Or, "Jeff's accident may help us redesign our safety plan in better ways."

4. Achievement. At this point, I arrive at a successful resolution to the problem. This does not necessarily mean that the problem itself goes away. Instead, I have simply resolved my own difficult feelings about the situation. Occasionally, the resolution profoundly changes my external circumstances. At this point, I acknowledge that this difficulty was indeed a gift to me. Whether it changes my circumstances or merely changes me, I am moving ever closer to the person I was meant to become. I now view my own experience with burnout in this way.

Because of my struggle, I've experienced a unique opportunity to speak to others struggling with similar issues. I've watched others change and grow. I've helped new physicians consider avoiding burnout before it begins. I've discovered gifts I did not know I possessed. What a joy this journey has been! I am honestly grateful for the many rewards I've experienced as a result of that dark and difficult season.

Burnout taught me that I have no control over the size of the waves, the conditions of the sea, the wind, or the weather. But I do have full control over my surfboard. Whenever I face difficulty, I can choose my attitude. When I choose wisely, I find I am able to enjoy a thrilling ride! It's up to me to swap my surfboard.

Chapter Eleven
CHARTING A COURSE: PREVENTING BURNOUT BEFORE IT BEGINS

"A bad beginning makes a bad ending."
Euripides (Aeolus)

Yale-trained psychiatrist Dr. Carl Hammerschlag spent more than twenty years providing medical care for Native American patients. In his book *Dancing Healers*, (HarperOne, 1989), Hammerschlag relates a story of his first meeting with Santiago, a man suffering with congestive heart failure.

"I didn't know that he was a Pueblo priest and clan chief. I only saw an old man in his seventies lying in a hospital bed with oxygen tubes in his nostrils. Suddenly there was this beautiful smile and he asked me, 'Where did you learn to heal?'" Assuming he had asked about his training, the physician answered, listing his medical credentials. Santiago's next question startled him.

"Do you know how to dance?" Santiago asked. After some discussion and further misunderstanding, the old priest informed him, "You must be able to dance if you are to heal people."

Many years later, the doctor wrote, "The old man's words ... resonated with me. The unending story of my work life has been to seek my own music and learn the appropriate dance steps. I don't have it all figured out yet. But I believe the old man is correct. Dancing and healing go together. In the native culture, the dance is an expression of the healer's connection to the Divine. Without that connection, the healer has little to give. That's what happened to me. Without that connection, I burned up, wore out, and lost all joy in the very work I loved most."

As it turns out, my story is very similar. Without genuine spiritual health—a connection to something bigger than myself—I lost my way. The work I loved turned into a burdensome, thankless obligation. Turning it around took time and effort. Now I long to help others avoid my mistakes by preventing burnout before it begins to take hold. The best prevention begins at the beginning, long before disappointment and frustration become the lens through which we view our work.

I recognized this important connection—between beginnings and burnout—when the Indian Health Service requested that their clinical directors share advice for new physicians serving the Native community. At first, I ignored the request. But later, I thought of a single idea. As I began to write that down, many other ideas came to me. Before long, that bit of inspiration left me with a full list of ten suggestions. I sent my ideas in but I've kept a copy for myself.

As I look back on my list, I realize these ideas address the medical community. But they can also serve the greater community of human service providers, no matter where we work. So, with the goal of helping you prevent burnout long before it starts, here are my top ten suggestions for beginning a position in any of the helping professions:

1. Do not try to change everything immediately. From the very beginning, you'll no doubt immediately recognize dozens of things that should be changed. You will have a vision for how things can be more efficient or more productive. To avoid your own frustration, remember that the organization you serve has evolved in the location where you find it. Likely, the staff has strong reasons for choosing to do things in their own way. At the beginning, you may not yet have enough information to understand their reasoning.

Years ago, we had a physician join our medical staff. He was deeply concerned that our pediatric and family services worked out of different locations. The exam rooms, waiting rooms, and staff areas were completely separate. Frustrated by the situation, he loudly voiced his opinion at every opportunity. Instead of asking why we were set up that way, he expressed endless disapproval and frustration.

He was correct; most clinics do operate as he suggested. However, our clinic had barely survived a long struggle over this very issue. We had come to our current status with a great deal of compromise. His dissatisfaction ruffled the hard-won status quo. Because he didn't understand the history behind our decision process, his continued criticism built a wall between him and his staff. Speaking without understanding, he became his own enemy.

2. Listen. Determine who the people with real influence are. Every organization has people with positions and titles. Officially, these are the decision makers. However, the real decision makers are rarely the ones who wield the most power. This is especially true in the Native American community. We once had an outsider decide to rearrange the physical design of one of our clinic areas. The designer had the approval of all the people with titles but had neglected to include the real power brokers—the least visible but most influential tribal members. By underestimating the importance of these opinions, the new design plan was jettisoned, with many hurt feelings in the process. It was an unnecessary loss.

I have heard of a nearby hospital where the physical therapy clinic was controlled not by the clinic director, but by a single therapist whose father served as chief of plastic surgery. This therapist wielded an invisible but very real power; no changes or suggestions occurred without this therapist's approval. When others tried to overrule her power, she simply took her complaints and observations to her father who exclusively supported his daughter.

3. Your first priority must be to build relationships and establish trust. This takes time and care. It frequently means that you must lay aside your own priorities in order to serve the priorities of your new community—even when they seem less than ideal. When I was studying for my master's in public health, I heard the story of a man who traveled to a Guatemalan village with the intention of improving their water sanitation. When he arrived, he asked the group, "What can I do to serve you? What do you most need?" The village elders met to consider the question and decided that they most needed a new soccer field.

For one month, this man served the village by clearing bushes and trees and leveling a large playing field. Only when the soccer field was finished, when they trusted the stranger, did the villagers ask the man, "What can we do to improve our health?" After extensive effort in building a soccer field, the health expert could finally address their most urgent health care need: clean water.

In the Native community, the most appropriate question is always, "How can I help?" This question has great value in every service position. I have learned that I rarely succeed by offering information or advice when the listener is not yet ready. Be patient; earn validity in the eyes of those you serve. Only then will you be able to use the expertise you bring.

4. When asked for help, build a team. The excitement often begins when others finally ask for your help. At this time, it might be tempting to engineer a solution and push it through. This is the Lone Ranger approach to service; it rarely succeeds.

The best solutions come as a result of team building and consensus. Real change requires that relevant team members buy in to your solution. I've found that the strongest teamwork occurs when team members believe they have designed the solution themselves. While there are hundreds of books available for team builders, they all require that you consider the opinions and suggestions of others. If you struggle with getting a group to follow you, perhaps one of these valuable texts might help you with team-building skills. Many blogs also offer helpful suggestions and lists of important books.

5. You must learn the language of the culture you serve. Even when you serve English-speaking people, there remains much potential for miscommunication. In many minority cultures, communication occurs obliquely rather than directly. In this environment, you must listen both to the words said and to the words left unsaid in order to decode the intended message. You must not only listen differently, but to communicate effectively, you must also learn to speak in ways that will be accurately heard.

In my early days serving Native Americans, I used to attend weekly department meetings. Confident that I could easily multitask, I used to show up with a tall stack of patient records, doing my charting as the meeting progressed. I believed that I was engaged and involved and at the same time completing my charting. One afternoon, after our meeting, one of my nurse managers approached me. "Dr. Shelton, do you need me to schedule more administrative time for you?"

I paused before responding. I knew she had no additional administrative time to give me. I had enough sensitivity to ask myself, *Why is she asking me this?* Later, I asked another colleague about the situation and learned that by working on charts during the meeting, I had disrespected my team. It would have been easy to misunderstand my nurse manager's question. Her intent was not really to give me more administrative time but to correct my behavior, which she accomplished in her culture's typically indirect style of communication

Some time ago, a mother came to me demanding that I fire one of our staff physicians. She told me, "He told my son that he was fat and was going to die of diabetes." The mother, who had not been present at the doctor's appointment with her sixteen-year-old son, seemed to have a very clear picture of what had been said. I promised I would look into the situation.

As it turns out, when her son appeared at his regular clinic appointment, he was severely obese—by more than one hundred pounds. He had developed a skin condition, more common in Native Americans, which often indicates the onset of insulin resistance, a condition which is regarded as a precursor for type 2 diabetes. It wasn't hard to envision what might have happened in that appointment to prompt this woman's complaint.

The doctor caring for her son had likely been concerned about the boy's weight and apprehensive about the early indications of approaching diabetes. No doubt the doctor had expressed those concerns in straightforward medical terms. His communication, though succinct and direct, might have been effective in other situations, in other clinics. In this culture, however, his words carried an underlying message of criticism he never intended. Though his words were correct, he had failed to learn to speak the language of the people he served. Because communication is such a critical part of all human service work, we'll talk more about direct and indirect communication in another section using this very example.

6. Make respect your primary focus. Giving and receiving respect is a strong value in our community. The perspective of feeling disrespected can be harmful to our health. As frequently happens in my work, I was once called to a local hospital by a frantic member of the nursing staff. One of our Native American patients, a seventy-five-year-old woman with diabetes and a gangrenous foot, had curled into a fetal position and refused all further treatment. Rejecting the very surgery that would save her life, she had stopped talking. Unable to make any progress, the staff had called me, hoping I might intervene.

I sat beside the woman's bed and asked simply, "What's the matter, Ellen?"

In a small voice, she answered, "They think I'm just an old, drunk Indian."

Through lengthy conversation, I realized that she had undergone the standard intake questionnaire by multiple staff members, including nurses, an intern, and a surgeon. As part of a regular medical history, each had asked Ellen if she drank alcohol. Though she didn't drink, she perceived that the question had been repeated because they *believed* that she did or that they *believed* that she drank excessively. In the process, she concluded that they thought she was just an old, drunk Indian woman. Feeling disrespected and unimportant, Ellen shut down, effectively ending all her care. Only through genuine understanding can these crises be avoided. Ellen soon agreed to have the necessary surgery and recovered.

The word *respect* comes from a Latin root meaning to look back or to look again. It involves the idea of looking deeply into another person's world without devaluing or judging them. The idea of respect includes tolerance and openness to another person's perspective, culture, and ideas. It involves the conviction that another person's ideas and perspectives are every bit as valuable as our own. Respect flourishes in civility and small kindnesses. It involves seeking understanding in spite of obvious differences. Respect does more than endure another's differences; respect celebrates those differences.

Today nearly every medical conference includes a course about cultural sensitivity. The problem with these courses is that those who take them often believe that they have achieved cultural competence. With this belief comes pride, which is usually followed by serious errors.

These kinds of courses frequently minimize the many layers of differences between people and cultures. As they ignore subtleties, they lead us to believe that the work of understanding is finished. Armed with this new information, some providers stop asking questions. They stop listening. I don't believe that we ever become fully competent in cultures other than our own—in the same way that we can never fully know our own spouse. Instead, we must approach those we serve with genuine humility, openness, and critical self-reflection.

I know of a nurse who finished one of these cultural sensitivity courses, where she had been taught that Native Americans were stoic about their pain. The nurse was caring for a female Native American who had just had a hysterectomy. The patient was in severe pain and asked for pain medication. Because the nurse believed she understood Native Americans completely, she refused the medication. What she had learned in class kept her from listening with compassion. Her pride kept her from recognizing that there are different kinds of pain—and that some are handled more stoically than others.

Respect approaches others with cultural humility, even when you have served that culture for many years. Humility genuinely wants to hear from others. This respect involves generous listening, the ability to be fully present to someone, and paying full attention to the words and the underlying messages being shared.

Generous listening involves listening with the heart.

It hears more than what is said. It involves respecting and accepting what the patient sees and believes as true. Generous listening does more than solve problems. It decreases the feeling of solitude and isolation. It affirms the worth of the individual.

Universally pressed for time, none of us—not teachers or law enforcement or social workers or medical professionals—think we have enough time for this kind of approach. Remarkably, generous listening can evoke answers that give us deeper insight as to how we can help, heal, comfort, and support. In that way, taking the extra time may help us avoid dead ends and ineffective approaches. When we are so busy trying to keep the schedule, get to the next call, and answer all the emails, we often miss the important clues that help us effectively solve problems.

Sometimes, in order to listen generously, I must open the door for communication. By carefully choosing the right questions, I generate more information and more listening opportunities.

While these openings work in the medical profession, they may also help other helping professions:

- Help me understand.
- Tell me about your illness.
- How would you like me to help?
- What is it that is bothering you?

I am not the first to discover the tremendous power of listening having learned this from others. In her book *Kitchen Table Wisdom* (Riverhead Trade, 1997), Dr. Remen says, "The most basic and powerful way to connect to another person is to listen, just listen. Perhaps the most important thing we give one another is our attention. A loving silence often has far more power to heal and connect than the most well intentioned words." In the same book, she quotes Dr. Bernie Siegel, author of *Love, Medicine, and Miracles*, who says about this issue, "I have become convinced that the doctor-patient relationship is more important in the long run than any medicine or procedure."

Respect in the form of openness and generous listening will go far in creating powerful relationships where you have permission to share the best of what you bring.

7. Always remember you are a guest in the community you serve. No matter how gifted you are, your continued presence in your community depends on the will of those you serve. As Tom Selleck often repeated on his hit show *Blue Bloods*, "I serve at your pleasure, Mr. Mayor." His character knows that his position as New York City's chief of police is tenuous at best. The same is true for you. Your influence in any community depends on your ability to serve felt needs. If you insist on imposing solutions to problems the community may not even acknowledge, you will not remain in service for long. Serving others requires an attitude of genuine humility.

As for myself, I find that I serve best when I consider my contribution as an avenue of the Great Spirit who uses me, wherever I am, to meet the needs of others. This idea—that my work is sacred and that I am a tool in the hand of the Divine—enables me to lay aside my pride and trust that I will have what it takes to meet the needs I encounter even as I face them. In this way, I also trust that the Divine prioritizes the most important demands of those I serve. I need not impose my agenda on anyone.

8. To accomplish your task, you will need more than simple technical or professional skills. Look for those additional assets. No matter how well prepared you may be, you will need more than your education and training. In order to complete your work, you will need political, cultural, intuitive, and spiritual understanding. Some of these gifts are yours. Others belong to the people around you. If you believe that your work is a sacred calling, you can also believe that the Divine has placed additional resources nearby. Pay attention; look for those resources.

Perhaps your staff has a historical perspective that will help you provide services. You may need some political assistance. Someone nearby may understand your client population from a spiritual perspective. You will never discover or access these resources if you believe that you already know everything there is to know.

Humility admits need. Humility looks for and finds additional resources in order to accomplish the important tasks ahead. Sometimes we bump into these resources by making important mistakes, just as I did in our departmental meetings. Humility does not defend inappropriate behavior and attitudes. Humility learns lessons quickly and swallows the pride that lead us to make the same mistakes over and over.

9. No matter where you serve, take advantage of the resources available. The Indian Health Service has many resources to provide answers to questions and struggles. And other communities and helping professions have resources as well.

I know of a local police officer who recently responded to the murder of four fellow officers at a local coffee shop. Though he didn't know before he arrived, one of the officers had been a close, personal friend. He reports that in his twenty years of policing, this particular incident was the most horrific and difficult crime scene he had ever encountered. His department was keenly aware of the strain he suffered and offered a critical incident stress debriefing with a professional team. In spite of the machismo atmosphere of the police force—the I-can-deal-with-this-myself attitude—this officer attended the debriefing. He tells me that no one in the room wanted to be there. All of the officers involved were silent, withdrawn. "Even though it was very hard, and I didn't want to be there, the debriefing went well. I'm glad I went."

Some new jobs come with assigned mentors. Teachers have union representatives who can help with difficult staffing and parental issues. Members of the building staff may have insight about issues with the school's culture or staff. Social workers have supervisors, court representatives, and fellow staff members. Emergency responders frequently have chaplain services.

I encourage all new employees in every service profession to take advantage of any support system available. Do not be afraid to find whatever resources you require to maintain your balance. Do it before the pressure and frustration begin to take hold.

10. In order to serve for the long haul, you must nurture your spirituality. This, of course, is the central message of this book. I believe that developing spirituality is the most significant answer to burnout among those who serve people in difficult or stressful environments. When you begin to recognize that your work has a sacred element and that your presence in your community is no accident, you realize that you need more than simple intellectual knowledge and physical energy. You need spiritual energy. Spiritual energy comes only by nurturing your spiritual life.

As we have already said, spirituality and religion are not the same thing. Though religion can be a bridge to spirituality or an expression of spirituality, it is possible to be deeply religious without any genuine spiritual awareness. Don't let old patterns of religion or the habits of your upbringing fool you into thinking that you are spiritual.

Spirituality focuses on mystery and faith. It understands the importance of letting go. It realizes that the eternal and essential things cannot be quantified or observed under a microscope. Rather, the eternal and essential are often the least visible, though most important, things in life. Spirituality recognizes a reality that lies beyond matter and knowledge.

> Once again I am reminded of Albert Einstein's quote where he realizes: **"Not everything that can be counted counts, and not everything that counts can be counted."**

We nurture our spirituality by expanding our hearts to include purpose and meaning. As we do, we begin to value loving-kindness as a lifestyle rather than a virtue that we turn on and off as needed. We begin to see our existence and our work as purposeful rather than accidental. We recognize that what really matters are eternal things—the things we cannot see. We move from valuing ego (the things of the physical) to valuing essence (things like compassion, service, love, and relationships).

Nurturing our spirituality, we recognize that we are spiritual persons having a physical existence rather than the other way around. We value and seek divine guidance and presence, even as we serve others. As we pursue a deeper understanding of others—their thoughts, emotions, and perspectives—we express an empathy that releases a powerful neurochemical shift that enhances healing.

By attending to our spiritual health, we practice empathy more deeply in every encounter, both professional and private. We do this intentionally by creating space, stepping back from our frustrations and emotions, and moving towards others, recognizing their unique spirituality. As we do this, we ask for guidance, listening carefully for the voice we recognize to be bigger than our own.

This process can move one from being a technician to being a healer. Asking for guidance enables you to touch the people around you more deeply. As a technician, you deliver your training. As a healer, you offer so much more – compassion and empathy from a Divine source. Because of this, being a healer is not only more effective but also far more fulfilling.

This idea that one can be an instrument of the Divine is not new. It was expressed in the thirteenth century by Saint Francis and first published in its present form in 1912. You may have heard it as the Prayer of Saint Francis.

> Lord, make me an instrument of your peace;
> where there is hatred, let me sow love;
> where there is injury, pardon;
> where there is doubt, faith;
> where there is despair, hope;
> where there is darkness, light;
> and where there is sadness, joy.
> O Divine Master,
> Grant that I may not so much
> seek to be consoled as to console;
> to be understood, as to understand;
> to be loved as to love;
> for it is in giving that we receive,
> it is in pardoning that we are pardoned,
> and it is in dying that we are born to Eternal Life.

Saint Francis understood that effective healers considered themselves instruments. Some translations even use the term channel. In this context, our ultimate goal, according to Saint Francis, is to be the means by which Divine Love is transmitted to the people we serve. This requires that we have a spiritual connection to the Divine.

This may be what the old Pueblo priest meant when he told Dr. Hammerschlag, "You must be able to dance if you are to heal people." For the priest, the dance was his way of connecting to the Divine. It was this connection that provided the source for all healing, and he, through his dance, was the avenue for that healing.

And this then is the ultimate secret to moving beyond burnout to a life of joyful satisfaction. As one nurtures their connection to the Divine, they can find that place where they can be a conduit of divine love, without attachment, so that in bringing their gifts they are not used up but fulfilled.

Chapter Twelve
SPEAKING THE LANGUAGE

> "If people work together in an open way, with porous boundaries—that is, if they listen to each other and really talk to each other—then they are bound to trade ideas that are mutual to each other and be influenced by each other. That mutual influence and open system of working creates collaboration."
> Richard Thomas, actor, defining *collaboration*

I'd like to spare you, no matter where you serve, from living in dread of Monday morning, from the anguish of hating your job, from professional boredom, and from feeling endlessly used and emotionally worn out. I hope to help you keep the joy and creativity of serving people for the rest of your career. So far, I've emphasized how my lack of spiritual maturity contributed to my own burnout, but there were other factors as well.

MISCOMMUNICATION

Many of my frustrations evolved from miscommunication, both with my staff and with the people I serve. Though my intentions were good, I found that occasionally my words offended my patients and staff. Most of the time, I had no idea how my words might be considered cruel or thoughtless. And yet, somehow, I managed to annoy or irritate others. At the same time, my patients frequently spoke to me in what sounded like riddles, as if I should have to unravel their intended message with little assistance on their part.

At first, I believed that my struggle was an issue specific to Native American culture—something caused by a different communication style limited to that group. Desperate to understand the issue, I studied interpersonal communication; I tried to listen and respond more carefully. Still, the problem persisted.

As the years passed, I grew to understand that these misunderstandings were rooted in issues much larger than the population I serve. Similar kinds of miscommunication are commonly reported among many populations. I was not the only one experiencing these frustrations, and I particularly identified with the work of Cynthia Joyce from the University of Iowa, whose work on communication was published in the *Independent Voice*. (November, 2012 "The Impact of Indirect and Direct Communication") You may have discovered the ways that your communication style limits your effectiveness with the people you serve. Or perhaps miscommunication interferes with your ability to effectively serve with other team members.

When I first started working with the Indian Health Service, I brought my scientifically trained, fact-based language to work, assuming that others would understand and respond to that communication pattern. Though I learned to use common words for medical terminology, something was still missing.

I was polite and respectful, but my direct style seemed to put people off, creating distance and misunderstanding. More importantly, because I expected to receive information and connect with people in the same style of communication as my own, I found that I missed important messages from the people I served. I often failed to understand the real reasons behind patient visits.

Sometimes, my struggle was obvious. I might ask a new patient, "What's wrong today?"

Speaking the Language

To my bewilderment, patients rarely answered me directly. It was as if they wanted me to guess what bothered them. Someone might say, "My aunt thinks I should have my thyroid checked." With my fact-based approach, I discounted that statement and began looking for and asking about symptoms and problems. Because they had already expressed their concern, I rarely made much progress.

I learned that the Native American population seldom uses such direct communication. Instead, indirect communication is the norm. Rather than state their concern directly in the initial few moments of our visit, they broached subjects indirectly, mentioning a relative's concern rather than their own. This kind of approach is found in other populations as well.

The indirect communication style is common whenever a smaller, less powerful group communicates with a larger and more powerful group. You might see it among poor populations speaking with police authorities or with immigrant families speaking with school officials. It is especially common between majority and minority races. The minority group may use this indirect style in order to communicate information without offending members of the larger and more powerful group. It may also be the result of long-standing cultural traditions. I have observed similar difficulties while working with some Asian cultures.

Because the healing relationship, like so many other serving, protecting, teaching, and support roles, is critically dependent on effective communication, I believe that we must consider how differing styles interfere with our mission. Direct communication and indirect communication styles are inherently different.

Do you remember the story of the mother who came to me asking that I fire one of my staff physicians? Though she had not attended her son's doctor's appointment, she was offended that the doctor had told her son that he was fat and going to die. From the physician's point of view, her son had gained a significant amount of weight. He had a skin condition indicating he was at high risk for developing diabetes. Because diabetes brings with it life-threatening health implications, undoubtedly the doctor had expressed his concern in a direct, logical, and sequential style. Her son, who was used to a more indirect style, had heard a more drastic message. Contrast the doctor's direct style with that of Santiago in Carl Hammerschlag's book *Dancing Healers*.

Santiago's question, "Do you know how to dance?" is typical of the indirect style of communication. The healer's question had little to do with actual physical movement and everything to do with spiritual health. Yet, the Native healer chose not to ask the question directly. Instead, Santiago asked using a metaphor for worship.

Let's look more closely at these two styles of communication:

1. **Style.** Direct communication is linear and sequential, with traceable logic and connectedness. In contrast, indirect communication is often circular or oblique. The indirect style implies facts rather than states facts directly. Explanations often involve stories, parables, or comparisons. Santiago, the healer in Hammerschlag's book, asked a question that seemed baffling in that it was irrelevant to the conversation at hand. The doctor who had examined the sixteen-year-old Native student in our clinic had stated his concern in a direct, logical, and linear style. However, the boy and his mother found his approach deeply troubling.

2. **Location.** Direct communication tends to be found in dominant societies where there is a clear power structure. It is frequently used among peers. Indirect communication is found more in community-based cultures (frequently minority cultures) where relationships are more highly valued than power structures. When we consider how to share our message, we should be keenly aware of our situation, location, and audience.

3. **Purpose.** While direct and indirect communication both exchange information, they often do so with different objectives. Direct communication seeks to be both efficient and complete

in the way it informs, convinces, and educates. My clinic doctor used relevant facts to try to persuade his patient to change his lifestyle. It might have been efficient, but it was not convincing to an indirect communicator. Indirect communication is used to exchange information in a way that maintains the harmony and relationships of the community. Indirect communicators will go out of their way to transmit information without offending the listener. Using the metaphor of dance, Santiago was using indirect communication to gently invite Hammerschlag into a conversation about worship and spiritual connectedness.

4. Medium. Direct communication is quite literal, using words and terms that accurately reflect the meaning and content of the message. Indirect communication often includes stories and analogies. The indirect style uses all of the communication tools available and relies heavily on nonverbal communication, including facial expressions, eye contact, and body language. Pauses and silences, eye contact, and body position all convey important messages that must not be ignored. You can imagine the danger inherent in electronic messages with those who regularly prefer indirect communication. Electronics rarely convey these important nonverbal cues.

5. Value. Of course, both kinds of communication have their value. Direct communication has the advantage of accuracy and speed. Truth is given in complete doses, which, direct communicators assume, ensures that the message given is the message received. Indirect communicators value relationship above the message itself. They will sacrifice accuracy and speed in order to transmit a message in a way that protects or restores a relationship. Indirect communication may not transfer information as quickly or accurately (because it relies so heavily on interpretation), but indirect communicators hope that no one will be offended in the process.

6. Responsibility. The effectiveness of direct communication most depends on the skill and accuracy of the speaker. The speaker's precision determines whether the message is accurately received. Because indirect communicators share their message in a virtual code of story and anecdote, the responsibility for the message depends largely on the listener's ability to decode the words and associated body language, to read between the lines, and to discern the less obvious messages.

7. Perception and risk. To the indirect communicator, a message given directly can be perceived as rude or inappropriate—as it was by the boy in our clinic. As the indirect communicator looks for underlying messages in direct communication, they may actually perceive the given information in an exaggerated or inaccurate way. In such cases, the risk is that the listener may become fearful, take offense, or even withdraw or sever the relationship. In our clinic, the mother of the boy was so offended that she responded in very direct demand.

The direct communicator may find the conversation of those who use indirect methods too difficult to discern, becoming frustrated as they wade through innuendo, analogy, and story. Direct communicators can become frustrated by the intensity of time and focus required to decode these messages. For those who use direct methods, the risk is that they misunderstand or cannot discern the message and give up conversation altogether.

8. Benefits. Direct communication has its benefits. Messages can be conveyed quickly and accurately, which is critical in emergency situations where every moment counts. Indirect communication has the potential to coalesce relationships. It can express care and concern in powerful but subtle ways. It engages emotions, giving it additional power to persuade or encourage. This may be especially important in long-term or chronic illness.

Considering these differences, you can see how these two very different styles might lead to miscommunication. More than once, the staff of our hospital has called me to intervene in serious misunderstandings. As I've gained understanding, I'm better able to help clarify the issues. Let me give you some examples:

I was once called to the hospital to help a patient who had been hospitalized the previous evening with hypertension. During the night, the patient had been unable to sleep, his blood pressure had continued to escalate, and he had become quite anxious. When I arrived, he was very agitated. Considering his health history, I didn't like this progression.

"What happened?" I asked him.

"They told me I'm going to have a heart attack and die and they are going to have to shock me back to life."

This poor man had spent the night anxiously waiting for his heart to stop. No wonder his blood pressure continued to rise! If I'd heard that message, I'd be anxious too.

It didn't take long to understand what had happened. During his admission, the medical staff had asked him about his "code status," in order to document his wishes should his heart stop. Because the patient did not understand the implications of the question, the hospital representative had carefully described the process of CPR, including resuscitation and defibrillation. From this simple question and explanation, which was nothing more than normal hospital admission procedure, the patient had interpreted that this event would actually happen to him during his hospital stay. His anxiety built with every passing hour. At which moment would the heart attack occur?

With much care, I was able to help him understand the nature of the question. Eventually, he calmed down. His is not the only case of misunderstanding.

I once referred a patient with an inguinal hernia to a nearby surgeon. My patient's general health was compromised by congestive heart failure, liver disease, and fluid buildup in the abdomen. After his referral, when I saw him again, he was surprisingly angry. He said, "If I were a young man, that doctor's scalp would be hanging from my teepee."

I asked what had happened during his visit with the surgeon.

"He said that if he operated, my guts would be all over the operating room floor."

I had to agree with my patient. This would certainly be an alarming message for anyone to hear.

I'm quite certain that my surgeon friend did not actually say this. More than likely, he had explained that the abdominal swelling, caused by fluid buildup, would make it difficult for him to close the surgical wound. The surgeon might have suggested that the swelling be relieved before scheduling surgery. My patient had clearly misunderstood the intended message. Instead, because he was used to indirect communication, my patient had ignored the words themselves, looking for the underlying, oblique message. The circumstance he envisioned was dire enough to cause great offense.

Notice too that my patient expressed his anger indirectly—using the analogy of the warrior and scalp. Even his response to the surgeon's message was conveyed through a word picture. These are normal communication snafus experienced between direct and indirect communicators. It's no wonder that emotions rise as messages become garbled.

In another case, I cared for a woman with chronic obstructive pulmonary disease. She had been a lifelong smoker; however, with much persuasion, we had helped this woman cut back to one cigarette daily. Still, she struggled with diminished lung function.

I wondered what more might be done and referred her to a pulmonologist. Not long after her appointment, my nurse asked me to see the patient again. I found she had grown much worse. I asked about her appointment with the specialist.

"All he did was scold me for smoking," she said. The appointment had left her so distressed that she had gone back to smoking a pack of cigarettes every day!

It didn't take much to imagine how the appointment had gone. More than likely, the pulmonologist had begun by taking an accurate medical history and noted that she was still smoking.

He probably advised her that she would do better if she quit. However, as an indirect communicator, my patient had heard his advice through ears used to the indirect style. His simple, direct message would have been interpreted as having much larger implications, so she thought that she had been scolded, shamed, and disrespected. In her discouraged and disrespected state, she ended up smoking even more.

This issue of direct versus indirect communication is important because communication is central to all of us who serve the public and is especially important to health-care providers. Without awareness, we frequently misunderstand one another and fail to deliver the very information we want to provide. In the process, we may offend those we serve, distressing them so much that they are less willing to listen and cooperate. Simply by speaking in a language that others do not understand, we diminish our influence with the very people we hope to help.

AWARENESS

Understanding begins with awareness. Once you understand the differences in these styles, you can begin to look for clues about the communication method being used. With indirect communicators, try to avoid blunt or accusing statements—even when you consider them true. "You are overweight," would be better expressed, "Have you considered how much better you might feel if you lost a few pounds?"

FEEDBACK

Recognize that with the indirect communication style, you are less likely to get what you would consider to be accurate feedback. In the process of adjusting care or assessing efficacy, you may have to change the way you seek information. A direct question may not elicit a direct response. This may be true in social service, education, public safety and other professions as well. Of course, every professional avoids expressing frustration under these conditions. However, with indirect communicators, your body, facial expressions, and posture may betray your emotions. Work hard to avoid communicating your frustration or disapproval.

THE POWER OF A QUESTION

Be careful to ask enough questions to elicit the whole story, making certain you have all the information you need before you act. Try to begin with open-ended, inviting questions, progressing to more delicate issues as your client or patient opens up.

As you seek information, be patient. If you have a direct style and work with indirect style populations, you will soon realize that most interactions take longer than you like. Allow for extra time. Your ability to help under these circumstances requires it. In the long run, accommodating and allowing for these differences in communication styles is more efficient than the managing the confusion which arises when you ignore them.

Here again, open-ended phrases like these can be very helpful:

- Help me understand.
- I'm not sure I understand what you are saying.
- Tell me more about …

Whether or not you work with a minority population, work hard to study the language and communication styles of the people you serve. When you adjust your style, accommodating for cultural differences, you may find that you are able to reduce a great deal of the stress you encounter every day. In the end, you will be more effective in accomplishing the very work that you love.

Chapter Thirteen
BOUNDARIES

> "People who own their lives do not feel guilty when they make choices about where they are going. They take other people into consideration, but when they make choices for the wishes of others, they are choosing out of love, not guilt; to advance a good, not to avoid a bad."
> Henry Cloud and John Townsend, *Boundaries: When to Say Yes, How to Say No, to Take Control of Your Life*

After all of my presentations, I try to allow time for audience questions. During one of these discussions with a group of medical residents, a woman raised her hand.

"You want us to be fully present, and I do that. You want us to have spiritual practices, and I do that. This stuff is all very well and good," she said. "But it doesn't change the facts. The truth is that we are forced to manage very complicated medical issues in fifteen-minute appointment blocks. And not only that, but medical school expects us to learn and retain vast amounts of information in a completely unrealistic time frame. No spiritual practice will change that."

She had barely finished speaking before the audience burst into applause.

Clearly, her complaints struck a chord of truth with her classmates. Of course, she was right. I tried to help her see that building a healthy spiritual life would help her face these difficulties from a peaceful, calm place. While a spiritual practice doesn't change the world around us, it does change the way we approach the world. Afterward, I felt that I hadn't quite given this woman my best answer, and I wrote a letter to her class in order to express myself more clearly. In essence, I explained:

> It is true that the purpose of a healthy inner life is to face difficulties with a calm resilience. However, this is not to say that we always peacefully accept the status quo or those things which are unjust or unhealthy. Peace, by itself, is not enough and falls short of the true goal of the tool. By using the tools (mindfulness, gratitude, forgiveness, and divine guidance), I seek a place of resonance. Doing this, I stop drinking the poison of resentment and reactivity. As I step back and experience peace and seek divine guidance, I open myself to the divine wisdom available to help me find my best way to address the problem.
>
> In the face of unacceptable conditions, I use the tool to access the deepest source of wisdom available and follow that by making a plan or strategy in conjunction with the wisdom I am given. Often those things that catch our attention and make us most likely to react are the very things we are called to address. Wisdom may call us to advocacy, organizational change, or legal action. It may lead us to form a group to address an issue or to ask for change from supervisors. It may, over time, change the kind of work we do or the focus of the clients we serve.
>
> The wisdom we seek is unlimited in its ability to direct us toward solutions we cannot imagine in a reactive, angry state. Over the years, I have

found that action coming from a place of love and wisdom is much more effective than action coming from reactivity. I have experienced many of these moments in my own life.

While having a healthy inner life gives us peace, it does not make us doormats. Spiritually authentic people don't say yes to every request. In fact, the stronger we are spiritually, the more likely we are to find ways to say no in a healthy way. Today, this ability (to say no in healthy ways) falls under the purview of boundaries, a term which has become a cultural buzzword.

From my perspective, burnout and boundaries come together when the work environment asks those in the helping professions to perform in ways that don't reflect their personal beliefs or standards. Most often, these demands involve providing substandard or impersonal care. You might recognize some of these requests:

- A social worker is asked to manage more foster placements than appropriate.
- A doctor is asked to treat patients according to insurance coverage rather than best medical practice.
- A patient asks for an early refill on a pain medication.
- A police officer is asked to take additional shifts because management hasn't hired enough officers.
- A teacher is asked to manage an overfilled classroom.

As we comply with these requests, we compromise our own deeply held values and standards. Each of these experiences has the potential to leave us feeling resentful because we have conceded something important in ourselves. The social worker responsible for too many children feels that none of the children are receiving adequate supervision. Because doing her best work reflects her deepest values (the value of helping at-risk children), her workload begins to sap her sense of integrity. Taken together, these experiences chip away at our identities. Before long, we feel disillusioned, discouraged, even depressed.

All of this fuels burnout.

These challenges are part of my everyday experience. A coworker asks me to take his on-call night because he hasn't planned ahead. A patient asks for a bronchodilator even though she continues to smoke. My staff asks me to squeeze in an extra patient, even when that patient failed to show for his last appointment. On my day off, I got a text from a patient requesting antibiotics. She didn't want to go through routine clinical procedures to be evaluated; she wanted me to care for her, even though I was not the physician on call.

Most of us view these kinds of interactions as awkward or frustrating. We feel as if we can't win. Saying no may make us uncomfortable or, worse, may result in unpleasant consequences. If we say yes, we feel resentful, as though others have taken control of our important choices. We may feel used, as though others have taken advantage of us. Unless we do something, resentment simmers and relationships deteriorate. We begin to dread interactions with coworkers and employers. We may even avoid family members when we know we will have to disappoint them.

Sometimes our discomfort with saying no begins long before we initiate our professional lives. Driven by childhood wounds, people with boundary issues are sometimes desperate for the approval or the attention of others or for reward or success. For them, saying no entails big risks. Saying no might end relationships and keep others from liking or loving them. Saying no might turn the boss against them. It might keep them from the next promotion or award.

For people with boundary issues, the risk of rejection is so real and so powerful that they would rather surrender their lives to the demands of others than face the potential consequences. Defining and defending boundaries is too taxing, too overwhelming, or too threatening. As a result, these people become overly compliant, feeling resentful and stressed and struggling in many areas of their lives.

I remember a past colleague who struggled with boundary issues. He had trouble managing his staff, who refused to take direction from him. He had difficulty maintaining a professional relationship with his patients, who manipulated him into treatments he would not have chosen. He had difficulty saying no to his own teenagers. As a consequence, everyone found this professional easy to control. From my viewpoint as an outsider, it seemed as if he were a puppet dangling from the cleverly manipulated strings of a puppeteer. Depending on who held the strings, this person danced exactly as directed. A servant to all, his stress level seemed too high to survive for long.

Compromising our values bears consequences too serious to ignore. As we've already discussed, the stress of resentment and anger brings with it the dangers of high blood pressure and heart disease. When we acquiesce to unhealthy demands, we sometimes compromise the health and safety of others, including patients and team members. Sometimes, in the process of coping with the unreasonable demands of others, we place additional, equally unreasonable demands on those who work for us—our nurses, professional assistants, and partners.

When team members ask us to overlook their own addictive or destructive behaviors, we put others at risk. As we give in to others, we sacrifice the health and well-being of the team itself. In interpersonal relationships, compromising our deeply held values can create wounds that last for a lifetime. These important consequences demand that we establish and keep healthy boundaries. For those of us in the helping professions, I call this saying no in a good way.

SAYING NO IN A GOOD WAY

What is a boundary? For our purposes, I use this definition: boundaries are the rules you establish that enable you to live out your most deeply held values.

Let me give you some examples: If honesty is one of your deeply held values, you will likely establish a rule that deals with telling the truth. If maintaining family relationships is one of your deeply held values, you will likely live by rules that govern your priorities about family events and time together.

Here is a key point: no one can determine your values for you. A single teacher may express different values than a married teacher with four children. In the same way, no one can tell you which rules express your individual values. For that matter, no one else can determine which values you will prioritize at any particular period in your life. A father with a newborn child might have different priorities than one whose children have all grown and left home. As our lives change, our responsibilities evolve, and our families grow, our priorities will likely change as well. How you express your values will be reflected in your own unique choices.

For some professionals, family values might translate to this rule: "I will always be home by six." For others, family values might mean: "I will always have a weekly date night with my wife." Whatever rules you choose, these become your boundaries. If you determine to protect those boundaries or rules from the demands of your workplace, they will keep your values safe from the interference of others. You will experience the satisfaction of living with integrity.

What you value determines what you do.

In order to have healthy boundaries, we must develop a strong sense of self and a clear understanding of what is important to us. This self-understanding doesn't come easily; it requires careful reflection. Sometimes, we recognize our values after making serious mistakes or experiencing difficult trials. A death. A broken marriage. A health scare. While these experiences may be unpleasant, they may help us to discover what is truly important.

No matter how long it takes to develop your own rules for living, you must protect those rules. I have learned through hard experience that no one will protect my boundaries for me. These rules exist so that I feel comfortable with my own behavior and so that my behavior reflects who I am in the deepest part of me. No one else has those priorities in mind. I am the only one who can protect these values.

As people in the helping professions, protecting our boundaries can be especially difficult. After all, when others need help, they turn to us. In fact, helping others might be one of our most treasured values. Our ability to solve problems—whether they come from feuding neighbors, learning disabilities, or ill patients—becomes part of our identities. We field difficulties, mend fences, and generate solutions. This important value—this *helper* value—can actually interfere with our ability to create and protect the boundaries that represent our most deeply held beliefs.

When we are confronted with difficult requests, our response is often far more complex than a simple yes or no. As professionals who work in teams, we respect the value of a team player. We want to be responsible team members. We want to help other team members, and we hope they will reciprocate when necessary. But when requests come to us over and over again or when we feel others are taking advantage of us, we can struggle with guilt over saying no and feel deepening resentment when we say yes.

Sometimes, even when we make a decision that is right for our values, we experience the additional pressure of a coworker (or patient or client) who won't take no for an answer. These people often resort to guilt, persuasion, or manipulation to force us to change our minds. Some bosses may threaten us, either overtly or subtly. You've probably heard things like these:

- If you don't do this, we'll be understaffed. Someone could get hurt.
- This little girl won't have any place to stay if you don't take her.
- I've never seen a patient this sick. You wouldn't want her to go through the weekend without being seen.
- I wouldn't want to write this up in your employment review.
- You're the only doctor who cares about my pain.

When a patient begins a conversation by stating, "You're the best doc I've ever had," and progresses through a long series of compliments, I know what is coming and try to prepare myself. Sure enough, these compliments almost always precede an inappropriate request for pain medication. Fortunately, with much experience, such obvious manipulation is easier to resist.

Still, it can be a hard place, that tight squeeze between yes and no. And when my emotions are high, when I don't take time to step back and think, and when I don't seek help from the Divine, I lose touch with my own creativity. Without using my tool, I am more likely to respond without first seeking another solution.

In my case, one frustrating compromise or one resentful yes can leave me cranky for the whole day. When these compromises begin to stack up, I find the joy of my work squeezed dry. When I say yes when I ought to say no, I focus my resentment on the object of my frustration. If this is a coworker, it can become difficult to be my old self around them. Instead, I'm stiff and formal. I've even found myself avoiding interaction with those who have taken advantage of me.

Rather than managing a consistently abusive boss or coworker, some people manage by getting out or finding another job. Unfortunately, because they have never established healthy boundaries, the problem goes with them to their new positions. Those who take advantage of others are remarkably quick to spot and approach those who don't defend their boundaries well. These, they assume, are the people who will do their work, cover their mistakes, and make up for their own deficiencies. I didn't want to be the one on whom others preyed. Neither did I want to live a life filled with resentful yeses. If there was some other possibility, I had yet to find it.

In truth, most boundary issues can be solved without resorting to two very limited responses—yes or no. After years of frustration, I've discovered that in nearly every case, the tool can help me uncover a third option—one that rarely presents itself without taking a step back.

As in all other situations, my first step is to create space and step away from my emotions about the situation and the need for an immediate decision. When I am asked for an on-the-spot response, I answer with some variation of the following:

- Let me think about that.
- Could I get back to you with a decision about this?
- I'm in the middle of something. Can I call you back in a few minutes?
- I'll let you know as soon as I have a chance to check with my schedule.

These kinds of phrases relieve the pressure to respond immediately. They give me time to take a deep breath, focus myself, and be aware and fully present. I use the time I've gained to step back. I give thanks in the midst of the situation, perhaps for the unique opportunity to interact with this person or consider this obligation, perhaps even for the opportunity to strengthen my commitment to my own values. If I'm feeling taken advantage of or overlooked in the request, I deliberately forgive the insult.

When I have stepped away from my own emotions and am quiet and aware of myself, I invite the Divine into the situation. I take a deep cleansing breath and ask for wisdom and guidance.

At this point, almost miraculously, I become aware of a third choice—something that lies somewhere between yes and no—something that will satisfy all the parties and still allow me to protect my values. The third plan allows me to avoid the guilt of saying no, while at the same time giving me a creative way to express my values, honoring the deepest sense of my own integrity. In the process, I am energized and enabled to give a generous and compassionate response. I am not left with a resentful yes.

Let me show you how this might work. More than once, I've been asked to take another physician's on-call schedule. Sometimes, it happens because another team member hasn't managed his own obligations well. When I repeatedly do more than my fair share in the clinic, I'm tempted to feel resentful. When I say no, I often feel guilty. But when I step back, use my tool, and let the Divine guide me into a wise compromise, the solution is often better than either yes or no.

I might say, "I can take call for you this weekend, but I'll need you to take my holiday weekend in return."

To a patient wanting to avoid the clinic routine, I might say, "I can call that prescription in for you, but I'll need you to stop by the office and let the nurse take some blood. Then you'll need to schedule an appointment for follow-up."

When my boss asks me for more work than I can complete in my normal workweek, I might say, "I can finish that report this week, but I'll need to postpone something else. Which of my responsibilities would you like me to delay?"

I've found that some of my staff are better at defending their boundaries than others. Recently, one of our specialists was asked to help train our residents. She agreed to this new responsibility under the condition that she be given some additional weekly hours of administrative time. It was a yes that felt good to her and one that allowed her to complete the training task without compromising her ability to complete her other work to her own high standards. On her part, it was a wise decision.

Boundaries

In my recovery from burnout, I've had to work on establishing and protecting my boundaries. As I've grown, I have begun to recognize and respect the boundaries of those around me. For instance, when I ask something extra of someone on my staff, I now begin by offering some benefit for the additional request, perhaps offering compensation time, and I try to give my staff permission to say no, even explaining, "You don't have to do this, but I wonder …"

When one of my staff gives more than is expected, I try to reward their effort in some significant way. Above all, when someone tells me no, I am quick to affirm their choice. "That's fine. I understand that you need to get home to your family."

I appreciate these compromises because they reveal generous and compassionate responses to the requests I encounter without leaving me resentful or frustrated. Many of the examples I've given don't seem terribly inspired. However, more than once, I've recognized inspiration that was far wiser than anything my own experience might suggest.

I don't want to imply that every conflict can be solved by compromise. In some cases, boundary issues can lead us to find creative solutions that require far more effort than a simple compromise.

I know of one physician who worked for ten years at a community clinic. Over time, he became more and more frustrated by the administration's control over appointment times, which were too short to manage care for his complex patients. As his resentment built, he recognized that the situation violated his own value of quality patient care. He was providing Band-Aid medicine, and burnout was not far off.

He could simply have quit the job. Instead, he began to look for a place where he could concentrate on keeping patients healthy rather than focus on treating illness. Unable to find such an environment, he got creative. This conflict over short appointment times eventually led him to innovate an entirely new paradigm of medical treatment. Now, he works in an environment that rewards providers for keeping patients healthy, and my friend feels better than ever about his work.

This issue of boundaries and using the tool to find creative, healthy ways to say no will not come easily to everyone. However, if you wish to avoid burnout, you will need to give it some attention and practice.

Chapter Fourteen
THE IMPORTANCE OF COMMUNITY

"Maybe the real issue here is that we were not created to do life by ourselves. We were not given a sentence of solitary confinement and placed in a world of isolation, but from the moment we entered this human experience, it was clear there was a world waiting to be discovered, creatures which were there for our interaction. And the spark inside us often has to be spoken to, to be touched by the soul of another."
Stephen Lovegrove, *How to Find Yourself, Love Yourself, & Be Yourself: The Secret Instruction Manual for Being Human*

In her delightful book *Kitchen Table Wisdom*, Stanford Medical School faculty member and pediatrician turned counselor Dr. Remen introduces a powerful story with these words:

> At one point two surgeons who were respected faculty at a nearby medical school were both patients of mine in my counseling practice. Each had come because of loneliness, depression, and burnout. Neither was aware that the other was also here seeking help.

Remen reveals that both these physicians struggled with feelings of defeat when things went badly in the operating room or when they lost patients. Both wondered why some patients did well, while others in the same condition did not. Both wondered about their choice of career and about the profound sadness they felt on the death of their patients. Both expressed deep loneliness. Though these two surgeons shared an office, a receptionist, and a waiting room, neither had ever discussed these difficult feelings with the other.

As their therapist, Dr. Remen could not inform either surgeon that she was treating his partner. Still, she frequently suggested they speak to one another about their struggles. She always got the same response.

"Him? Heavens, he would just laugh."

This true story illustrates our reluctance to share our pain when work becomes overwhelming. At the same time, it demonstrates the power of isolation to amplify the symptoms of burnout.

All our feelings of frustration, grief, overwork, and disappointment are magnified when we believe that we are the only ones struggling with these feelings. However, when we share our difficulties, brainstorm solutions for common problems, and encourage one another in growing our spiritual health, we create an environment where burnout is less likely to overwhelm us. In a healthy community, we are more likely to begin and sustain new habits of all kinds, including those of a spiritual nature.

In a study conducted by the National Weight Control Registry, researchers found those who lost weight and attended a support group twice monthly kept their weight off. Those who did not have support gained half their weight back in one year. The power of support has been demonstrated in many addiction and alcohol recovery programs.

The reverse is also true. Negative attitudes and responses can be passed on through community as well. Doug, a police officer in a large West Coast city, told me that he easily recognized other officers struggling with burnout.

"They tend to congregate together, sharing their frustration and negativity. I could almost see them spiral downward. It started with the common complaints—about hours, shifts, and regulations. Then they began to believe that what they did made no real difference."

Before long, these complainers were the ones getting into trouble. Their poor attitudes showed in their interactions with the public. The public filed complaints about them. Things continued to deteriorate until they resented the brass and held deep grudges against department leaders.

"You can tell who they are," Doug said. "They are the ones who think everyone else is the problem. Their us-against-them mentality leaves no room for negotiation. For them, burnout eventually led to leaving the force."

Policemen are not alone in this tendency. I have heard teachers report that negative staff members often congregate together in the lunch room, complaining and whining. It happens in staff rooms everywhere.

Doug refused to hang out with these cops. "I avoided them. In fact, I rarely spent time with off-duty officers."

Instead, Doug shared the struggles of his police work with a close group of guy friends who knew him well. Together, they worked to support his vision of serving people with the help of the Divine.

I too had a group who helped me in my most difficult season. Like Doug, my group didn't consist of other medical professionals. I was part of a book club; ostensibly, we met to discuss the books we read. At the same time, though, we became a part of one another's lives. We talked. We told the truth about how we were feeling and about what was happening in our individual worlds. We really met to talk about how we were coping.

In spite of the fact that no one in my group understood the problems of medicine firsthand, they did know me. They cared about me and my frustrations, and they helped me sort out ideas that might lead me in a new direction. Though we hadn't met for this purpose, this community of men played an important part in helping me climb out of burnout.

The people in my book club had internalized the idea of serving the Divine by serving other humans. I valued the support I received so much that I eventually began a book club with my medical residents. Together, we read and discussed books about the human side of medicine—the connection side. Through those book discussions, we gave one another permission to ask the more important question: "How is it going?"

In the context of the book club, I found that residents felt safe enough to share a problem or struggle. They expressed frustration or shared advice with a younger colleague. Though the books were helpful, it was the discussion that allowed us to support one another in more meaningful ways.

As you've read through this book, you might have recognized others in your professional workplace who struggle. By forming your own group, you might help yourself assimilate your new practices. The reason for your gatherings need not be directly related to developing your spiritual life; however, with careful thought, you might make that a part of your professional support. Together, you might strengthen one another, arming yourselves against burnout. It's worth considering.

Over the years, I've watched many groups interact. During their years together, the residents in our program form a kind of support group. Some groups seem to cultivate negativity. They share frustration in a way that amplifies their emotions and limits their options.

But recently, a group of family practice residents chose a different way. After a presentation about research regarding the importance of positive emotions in an emergency room, the residents began to consider how their feelings and thoughts influenced their attitudes, creating an environment that may or not reflect the realities of the world. These residents internalized the message of the study and decided to add something new to our routine of morning report.

The Importance of Community

Normally, this part of the workday can be very stressful. During report, the residents present the admissions and treatment plans from the night before. They receive new assignments or consider patients with complex medical issues. The process can generate overwhelming stress for these young professionals.

This particular group decided to require each resident to answer a daily question posed by the on-call resident. The on-call physician would pose a question designed to evoke a positive response or reflection. We heard questions like, "What's the best thing that happened yesterday?" Or, "What do you most look forward to this month?" Or, "What are you looking forward to this weekend?" The specifics of the question weren't nearly as important as the fact that the question elicited a positive response from the residents. They might ask about a plan, a goal, or a pleasant or satisfying memory.

I didn't think their plan would make much difference; however, I let them take the initiative. What could it hurt? To my surprise, I began to see a remarkable shift in our morning report. I noticed that there was more laughter and a stronger sense of connection between the physicians. The meetings became lighter. I could almost sense joy among the residents. At first, these changes were subtle. Later, though, during one morning meeting, I realized just how far we had come.

Six months after they had added the daily reflections, the resident on-call asked this question: "What are you thankful for?" One by one, the group responded. One resident shared that he was grateful to be with this particular group. He had endured a particularly difficult year, which included emotional difficulty that had nearly ended his career. In the process of responding, the resident started to cry. The other physicians came forward, offering hugs of support. Another resident mentioned that he had had to repeat a rotation and appreciated the support of the group during that difficult experience.

That morning report—unlike any I had ever experienced—was profoundly moving. Ordinarily, medicine is a highly competitive work environment where the stress of caring for patients is amplified by the drive to appear competent, confident, and unruffled. The work is demanding, and the responsibility for sick patients can be overwhelming. Somehow, simply by sharing a small moment of positivity, this incredible and creative group of residents had broken down the façade of image building and restored humanity to their profession.

Spending a few minutes every day sharing a positive emotion, that group transformed themselves into a supportive and encouraging team. It was something I'd never experienced before. Whether it was the optimism shared or the group support itself that changed those meetings, I cannot be sure. Perhaps it was both.

Today, reflections continue as a daily aspect of our morning report. It has become very powerful for our residents, improving their performance, as well as their cohesion as a team. Compared to the consequences of sharing negative emotions, this tradition has shown remarkable benefits among our team members.

Thoughts have the power to trigger an emotional response. Emotional responses, especially negative ones, have the power to trigger behavior—being curt with others or lacking empathy, for example. Bad behavior solidifies into habits. These behavioral habits can lead to further frustration, discouragement, resentment, and cynicism. All by themselves, negative thoughts have the power to start us down the path toward burnout. They deplete our creativity and interfere with our ability to solve problems. Perhaps the single positive thought generated during our reflection session was enough to stop the progress of negative thinking.

Much has been said about the danger of negative thinking. However, there is much power in the group support of a positive community. There is profound strength and influence in a group who likes you enough to be with you, listen to you, and encourage you. I once experienced this power in a most remarkable way.

Years ago, I was invited to participate in a Native American sweat lodge ceremony. In this ceremony, people come to the sweat lodge to pray to the Great Spirit for help with their troubles and to seek guidance. During the ceremony, held in a tiny hut, participants sat around a center pit where red-hot rocks had been placed by the fire tender. When the time was right, he poured water over the rocks, and steam filled the air. I entered this lodge to find a hot, dark place filled with strangers. With open hearts, we shared a common longing for God and for each other. After a time of silence, the leader indicated that we would go around the group and give each participant the opportunity to pray.

As each person spoke, these strangers began to share their souls. I was astounded by their complete, even brutal honesty. One by one, they cried as they shared their troubles, their hang-ups, and their deepest fears. The leader offered no solutions or answers to these problems. Instead, we simply brought these concerns to the surface, admitting our difficulties and needs. I found the ceremony profoundly moving. In this community of broken humans, we found healing.

A positive group has great power to influence the growth of our spiritual lives. In some professions this is more difficult than others. As many police officers have told me, the machismo image and the I-can-do-it-without-help facade can be hard to overcome. Even when group support is offered, many police, fire, and emergency personnel refuse to participate.

However, if you want to avoid or resist burnout, the support of others can be tremendously helpful. Your group need not be large or formal; perhaps you can simply invite a friend or two to join you for coffee. You do not need to study written material or lead discussions. You don't even need experience to lead such a group. With compassion and understanding, you can strengthen one another for the difficult task of serving people wherever you work.

Chapter Fifteen
A PATH TO JOY

> "Do not be afraid nor dismayed because of this great
> multitude, for the battle is not yours, but God's."
> 2 Chronicles 20:15b; New Living Translation of the Bible

There is one ancient Hebrew tale that captivates me. Though I grew up attending church and Sunday school, I don't think I ever heard this story in church. As I look back, I am surprised by this. The details of this story reveal important truths for all of us who face overwhelming stress—no matter what your religious or spiritual affiliation.

According to the story, there was once a Jewish king named Jehoshaphat. He ruled over ancient Israel, which then, as now, occupied a geographically desirable location with important port access and trade routes. Because of this, his people lived under constant threat of attack from other, more powerful kingdoms. One day, the king received word that a great army, formed by three nations, was headed toward Israel with intent to conquer his little country. The situation represented certain disaster. Knowing his army could not withstand such an attack, fear threatened to overwhelm the king.

With no military options, this king called on his people to join him in fasting and prayer. At the community prayer gathering, a prophet began to speak. "Do not be afraid! Don't be discouraged by this mighty army, for the battle is not yours, but God's ... Take up your positions; stand firm and see the deliverance the Lord will give you."

This phrase, "stand firm and see," appears in many forms throughout ancient Hebrew tradition. In most cases, it means, "Stand still and watch what God can do." Given this tradition, such a command would not have surprised the king. After giving thanks for this insight, Jehoshaphat consulted with his advisers and made arrangements for his army to go out and meet the enemy. The king decided to send a group of singers ahead of his army—singers whose only task was to sing songs of praise to God as the army marched toward battle.

Can you imagine being nothing more than a choir member when you discover that you have been chosen to lead the army into military battle? Their fear must have been nearly crippling.

After singing their way to the battleground, they expected to face the enemy army. Instead, Jehoshaphat and his warriors made a startling discovery there: as far as they could see, the dead bodies of enemy soldiers covered the land. Without a single skirmish, the enemy was completely vanquished. When Jehoshaphat's army went out to plunder the enemy, they recovered so much equipment, clothing, and valuables that it required days to collect it all.

The army experienced victory without fighting.

Not everyone takes this story literally. No matter what you believe, this story contains powerful truths for those of us considering the battles we face at work and in our private lives. You see, the message really focuses on the approach we use as we face difficulty. The great host challenging us may not be an army. It might be your boss or a particular patient or your workload. It might be a struggle in your marriage or with one of your children. The enemy in the story represents the one issue that seems completely overwhelming to you—the one problem for which you can find no easy answer.

In my deepest season of burnout, I totally identified with that ancient king. Even now, nearly every week there are times where my prayers sound something like this: "Oh my God, a great host has come against me." Please don't laugh! With great regularity, some overwhelming challenge comes along that defies my own problem-solving ability. Without a successful approach to these kinds of stressors, I would feel endlessly besieged, eventually growing discouraged and worn out. In time, I would lose my ability to bounce back, and I'd be on the fast track to burnout—again. These kinds of events—these successive waves of enemy armies—can have an additive effect, leaving most of us less able to cope, solve problems, or stay above water. Once we lose our creativity, even a simple problem can feel overpowering, adding to our stress.

In this story of an ancient king, we discover several simple steps for facing overwhelming difficulty:

1. Begin with your spiritual practice. When faced with bad news about the oncoming army, the people in the story immediately began to execute their spiritual practices of fasting and prayer. Just as our tools—gratitude, forgiveness, mindfulness, and guidance—shift us away from stress and alarm into our best selves, their spiritual practice also shifted them. Prayer and fasting reminded them that they were spiritual beings deeply connected to the Divine. Through prayer, they remembered the purpose and meaning in their existence, both as individuals and as a nation. Their spiritual practices reminded them of their divine connection and gave them confidence to move forward.

2. Let go. In the face of bad news, the king and his people lifted this overwhelming problem to the Divine and let go. This step fits our spiritual understanding, as expressed by theologian Richard Rohr in his book *Healing Our Violence Through the Journey of Centering Prayer*, where he states, "All great spirituality ultimately teaches about letting go."

Under ordinary circumstances, when we face an overwhelming problem, our knee-jerk approach is to let our egos direct our actions. Pride believes that whatever happens is a direct reflection of me and my inherent value. If there is a solution, it is up to me to discover it. In this self-directed paradigm, I am left to my own devices to solve all my problems. Pride takes credit for the good results and must take the blame for the bad ones as well.

Authentic spirituality, on the other hand, recognizes that we are not alone in our difficulties. It understands that at any moment, we can lift our problems into the hands of the Divine. This doesn't mean that we are absolved of action. Instead, we understand that we are no longer emotionally attached to the outcomes of our difficulties—whatever those outcomes might be.

Because the problem now belongs to the Divine, I need not fight to protect my reputation or position. I need not seek recognition or approval. Like the Jewish nation of old, I understand that this difficulty—this battle, this overwhelming problem of an oncoming army—belongs to the Divine. This is trust.

3. Seek guidance. In our story, the king has done his spiritual practice and received his assurance of God's protection, and then he takes the next step. As Jehoshaphat leads his army toward the battlefield, he receives additional divine guidance. As a result, he engages the most extraordinary battlefield strategy! What fool goes into battle putting his choir out front? Certainly this idea did not come from the king's imagination. Yet, no matter how foolish it appeared, the king acts on his divine inspiration or creativity.

There is another old Hebrew principle illustrated here. In Psalm 100, verse 4, the psalmist writes, "I will enter his gates with thanksgiving in my heart. I will enter his courts with praise." The psalm conveys the idea that thanksgiving will only get us so far. But praise moves us into the next place, creating additional space and moving us into a different state of consciousness where we can experience a deeper connection to the Divine. Perhaps Jehoshaphat understood that by leading his army into battle with songs of praise, his people would enter their best place—their most responsive place and a place where the miraculous might actually become possible.

While I have never commanded a country, or an army, I know what it is to face battles at work. Sometimes, these battles seem more like wars. The stakes are high; the consequences may even involve life or death. Other battles are more like skirmishes—struggles to keep the joy and passion in my work. Sometimes I battle just to feel like there might be something productive happening at my office. I battle to be a channel of blessing and to have meaning and purpose in my world.

I have found that praise is another step—another spiritual practice that moves me forward. For me, praise seems to be key to accessing the power of the Divine. Not only have I experienced this power myself, but I've watched others experience it as well. I've watched one specific set of parents face the battle of a daughter's addiction. While they might have wallowed in guilt or frustration that their prayers were not answered, instead they moved into praise.

Somehow, even in desperation and pain, these parents recognized that the addiction problem wasn't the whole story of their daughter's life; instead, it was only a small piece of her journey. They rejoiced that she was alive and that her addiction was part of some bigger puzzle. In gratitude and praise, they moved forward, able to listen for their next instructions. Their journey has been a remarkable testament to the power of praise.

Music helps me to take this step into praise. As I sing praise music, I experience a shift that moves me to the best possible place. My ego diminishes, and my desire to bring glory to the Divine takes its place. It is one thing to read words of gratitude and another to say words of gratitude, but there is tremendous power in singing out my thanks and praise.

We are only beginning to understand the power of music in the human psyche. A recent YouTube video titled "Man in nursing home reacts to music from his era," which has now been viewed by more than two million people, depicts the effect of music on an elderly man suffering from severe dementia. The man is nonverbal and nonresponsive when a volunteer brings an iPod to the man and places earphones over his ears. The music brings the elderly man to life; he sings, rocks, and taps his feet to the beat. In the video, the life-giving effect of music lasts long after the headphones come off.

After experiencing the music, this man engages in conversation, remembers parts of his past, and discusses the value of music. This music effect has been documented in many memory-impaired patients and speaks to the way that music bypasses the normal paths of brain activity. Perhaps this explains some of my spiritual connection with music, which others experience often, as well.

No matter how it occurs, after I have passed through gratitude, forgiveness, prayer, and praise, I begin to watch for synchronicity. Coincidences. Flukes. Happenstance.

And to my ever-surprised delight, I have seen the most amazing events. Relationships are mended. Patients improve. Staff squabbles disappear. Answers come to me. Doors open and sometimes close. But more than anything, I find that I am connected to a much bigger picture, a bigger goal, and a more significant purpose.

And in this, I find joy and meaning—the very things that prevent burnout!

A JEHOSHAPHAT MOMENT

These days I continue to experience Jehoshaphat moments. One occurred recently, and it illustrates how differently I experience stress when I engage my spirituality in the face of ongoing difficulty.

The tribe recently began a new medical endeavor. As medical director, this process has been deeply challenging. While I have some responsibility, the project does not belong to me; I answer to several committees who make the final decisions on major issues, including personnel. Most of the project development is currently in place. Most of the staff has been hired, and our new director has just resettled in our area. But my most recent challenge has been to find and recruit a staff physician with additional training and special interest in integrative care. We hired a medical recruiter to assist us. The recruiter required that we contact applicants only through him. My job was to interview and filter the applicants.

Not long ago, we invited a young oncologist to come for an interview. She had just completed a fellowship geared toward integrative care. After I spoke with her, she met with the team and with several of our committee members. In every way, she seemed the perfect candidate. I was ecstatic, certain we'd found our newest employee.

With her requirements for compensation, I went to our committee and made an argument on her behalf. Hers was a significant benefits package, and I wasn't sure that I could gain committee approval. To my surprise, the group agreed to hire her under her conditions. Convinced that we had found our perfect match, I made my offer to the recruiter.

Imagine my disappointment when the representative reported back to me; our offer was insufficient. Deflated and discouraged, I knew I could not return to the committee and ask for more compensation. They had already done the best they could do—far more than they had done for other equally talented candidates. In the language of their culture, they had made their last and best offer. To ask for more would be considered disrespectful.

Fighting my own emotions, I used the tool. Try as I might, I could not discover a creative solution. This baffled me as well. If only I could think of something that would swing the offer in our favor, but nothing came to me.

That night I couldn't sleep. Over and over, I considered our dilemma. At some point in the night, it occurred to me that like the old king, I had met the enemy. A great host had come against me. I had done everything I could; now I must let go and trust the Divine. I did this, using praise to help me make the shift. And then I decided to do one more thing. I would call the woman directly. Perhaps something I might say would convince her to reconsider.

I called her before work, but she did not return my call. I called again at lunch but did not reach her. After lunch, I attended a meeting. When I returned from the meeting, I found an email from the recruitment specialist. "Your candidate has contacted me and decided to accept your offer exactly as is."

I laughed out loud. Such joy! No matter how I had wrestled with the situation, no matter how I tried to intervene and to use my own wiles, I had not made any progress. But the Divine, who uses me to make a difference in my work and my world, had the solution all along. Minds were changed, and people moved as I had hoped. How exciting! And what a confirmation to me that this was the woman chosen to help us in the important work we do.

These are the kinds of adventures that await you. Your work life need not be characterized by defeat, discouragement, or disillusionment. You can restore the excitement and joy you once felt in your work.

The great thing about fostering your spiritual health is that it is a low-risk treatment for burnout. There are no negative side effects. You cannot overdose. Your only gamble is that you might find something deeper, something more meaningful, and something more rewarding to add to your daily experience. Perhaps you will discover something you've been secretly longing for your entire life. Perhaps your newly discovered spiritual health will enhance your interpersonal relationships as well. Perhaps as you learn to serve the Divine, you will grow in love for those most deeply connected to you. Perhaps you will discover a new joy and satisfaction in your home, in your neighborhood, and in your community.

If you choose to change your approach to your spirituality, you will likely discover that all of life changes. You may find yourself more fully present with those you love, more grateful for things you'd previously overlooked, and less bothered by petty frustrations and discouragement. Even the freeway may not be so bad!

What could be better than discovering that by nurturing your spiritual life, your whole life has become richer, more satisfying, and more generous? These side effects make the treatment even more worthwhile.

It is my hope that you discover new joy in work and life as you connect to and celebrate the spiritual in your world.

About the Author

DR. ALAN SHELTON

Dr. Alan Shelton lectures and teaches on the subjects of stress and burnout. He attended the University of Oregon Medical School, and completed his family practice residency at St. Francis Regional Medical Center in Wichita, Kansas. This was followed by a masters of public health from the University of Washington School of Medicine. Today, as a family practice physician, Dr. Shelton serves as clinical director at the Puyallup Tribal Health Authority, where he has worked in primary care for more than thirty years. He also has been involved in teaching Family Practice residents at the Puyallup Tribal Health Authority and at Multicare Hospital in Tacoma, Washington.

His own experience with burnout and recovery inspired him to share with others the essential role of spirituality in increasing satisfaction and fulfillment at work. His first book, *Transforming Burnout: A Simple Guide to Self Renewal* began this journey. In the ten years since its publication, Dr. Shelton has continued to focus on the topic of burnout, speaking to new audiences, gathering new anecdotes, and perfecting the techniques and skills all service professionals need to cope in today's new political and economic environments. He has compiled these added experiences and stories in this new book. Dr. Shelton feels blessed to be married to his wife, Shari, for 42 years, and very much enjoys spending time with his six adult children, their spouses, and six grandchildren.

BETTE NORDBERG, BSPT, RPT

Bette Nordberg graduated with a bachelor of science in physical therapy from the University of Washington. Sidelined by illness in 1990, she turned to writing. Since then, Bette has been published online, as well as in periodicals, drama venues, devotionals, and more than fifteen books—both fiction and nonfiction. Today, she also co-authors for writers who request her assistance.